MEMBERS OF PARLIAMENT FOR ANDOVER 1295 - 1885

A Chronological List with an
Introduction compiled by

R. ARNOLD JONES, BA

With a Preface by
Sir David Mitchell MP

Andover History and Archaeology Society
1996.

First published in 1972
by the Andover Local Archives Committee

Second revised edition published in 1996 by the Andover History
and Archaeology Society.

ISBN 0 903755 15 7

CONTENTS

ILLUSTRATIONS

Robert Dudley, Earl of Leicester.

Sir William Waller.

Richard Cromwell.

John Smith, - Speaker of the House of Commons.

Thomas Assheton Smith (the younger).

William Cubitt.

Sir William H. Humphery, Bt.

Henry Wellesley, 3rd Duke of Wellington.

The portraits of the Earl of Leicester, Richard Cromwell, John Smith and William Cubitt are reproduced by permission of the National Portrait Gallery, and that of Henry Wellesley, 3rd Duke of Wellington, by permission of the Duke of Wellington, KG, and Courtauld Institute of Art. The portrait of Sir William Waller is from G. N. Godwin's *The Civil War in Hampshire* (1904 edn); Thomas Assheton Smith from D. J. Croman's *A History of Tidworth and Tedworth House* (1991); Sir William H. Humphery from *Hampshire and Some Neighbouring Records, Historical, Biographical and Pictorial* (nd). The cover drawing showing Westminster and old Lambeth Bridge in 1929 is by Sydney R. Jones, from his *Thames Triumphant* (1943).

ABBREVIATIONS:

AA	Andover Borough Archives.
CSP Dom	Calendar of State Papers, Domestic.
DNB	Dictionary of National Biography.
Dod	Dod's Parliamentary Companion.
HCJ	House of Commons Journal.
HMC	Historical Manuscripts Commission.
PP	Parliamentary Papers.
Register	Register of the Unreformed Corporation of Andover - 1599 until 1835 (Andover Local Archives Committee, No. 7).
VCH Hants	Victoria County History of Hampshire.

I am honoured to be invited to write this Preface. The scholarly work of Richard Arnold Jones has produced an account of past Andoverian MPs which is both well researched, readable and informative.

It is fascinating to see his account of the unsuccessful demand of the populace of Andover to be allowed to elect their MP rather than have a limited number of Burgesses acting on their behalf.

Particularly startling is the discovery that the Earl of Leicester offered to pay all election expenses provided he could nominate the MP - even better asking for the election return to be sent to him blank so he could subsequently fill in the name! Securing his Lordship's nomination may have required a bit of intrigue but it was a lot less work than securing election as an MP today.

It is illuminating to find that Andover's MP John Smith held the office of Chancellor of the Exchequer for two years and subsequently, after much controversy, became Speaker. This was at the time of the Union with Scotland and hence Andover provided the first 'Mr Speaker' of Great Britain. Curiously he had first entered the Commons representing the rotten borough of Beeralston, a seat also represented by my thrice times great-grandfather.

The role played by prominent local families makes interesting reading. The Cubitts of Penton, the Wallops of Hurstbourne, the Paulets of Basing, the Jervoise family even then of Herriard (one of them sat for Whitchurch through seven Parliaments - not far short of my nine); more famously the grandson of the great Duke of Wellington was Andover's MP in 1874.

The Henley family are of interest. Robert was elected for Andover in 1679, his son Anthony in 1698 and his grandson, also Anthony, for Southampton - the latter being described, after he ran off with the 15 year old daughter of the Earl of Berkeley, as "noted for his impudence and immorality but a good estate". There is some controversy as to which of the Henleys wrote the following infamous letter to his constituents, generally ascribed to the Andover Anthony, when departing from Andover in 1700:

> "I received yours and am surprised at your insolence in troubling me about the Excise. You know what I well know, that I bought you and I know what perhaps you think I do not know, that you are selling yourselves to somebody else.
>
> But I know what you do not know, that I am buying another borough.
>
> And may God's curse light on you all and may your homes be as open to the Excise Officers as your wives and daughters were to me while I represented your rascally borough."

My research in the Commons Library suggests that although published in the local paper, the letter was probably a hoax attributable to his son. However, amongst the 180-200 letters a week, say 10,000 a year, I personally deal with there are a very small number where exasperation leads me to envy such freedom of expression ......

Finally, I am hopeful that at its next review the Parliamentary Boundaries Commission will have the good sense (which deserted it in 1995) to create again a constituency of Andover consisting of the town and all the surrounding villages which 'look to' it - villages which, as this archive demonstrates, have played a large part in the history of the town and its Members of Parliament.

David Mitchell
Andover's MP and
Member of Parliament for North West Hampshire
5th June 1996

AUTHOR'S NOTE

In 1972 the first edition of this work was published by the Andover Archives Committee, which since then has evolved into the Andover History and Archaeology Society, and I gladly take the opportunity of renewing my thanks to colleagues on the Archives Committee for their help, and especially to Mr J E H Spaul, who did much of the preliminary spade work, to the late Mr Melville Child and the late Mr G E Brickell, and also to the staff of the London Library for their unfailing co-operation. My thanks are also due to Mrs. Diana Coldicott for her help in preparing the second edition for the press.

I have been able to incorporate in this edition material which has become available in the last 20 years, particularly in the more recent volumes of the History of the House of Commons. It was gratifying to find the first edition in their monumental work.

I am grateful to Sir David Mitchell for providing a Preface and for giving me permission to quote from one of his recent speeches.

R.A.J.

I. MEDIEVAL MEMBERS

Representatives of Andover were summoned to nine Parliaments between 1295 and 1311, and attended six of them. All these assemblies included Prelates, Magnates, Knights and Burgesses, and in 1295, 1305 and the two Parliaments of 1307, the diocesan clergy were represented as well. For the most part, these Parliaments met at Westminster or London, the exceptions being that of 1301, which was summoned to Lincoln; the last of Edward I's reign, at Carlisle; and the first of Edward II's reign, at Northampton.

Andover, no doubt, owed its representation partly to its position on the main London to Plymouth road, and partly to the importance of its wool trade which, combined with its older history as a royal hunting centre, had led to the granting of charters from the reign of Henry II onwards.

Two members represented the borough in each of the six Parliaments concerned, but as John Arnoue sat in the two consecutive gatherings of 1306 and 1307 (and possibly also in the preceding Parliament of 1305 if he is the same person as the "Johannes Yarnyne" listed under that year) there are only 11, or perhaps 10, separate names. Some of these occur as witnesses to the early land conveyances, between 1291 and 1311, preserved in the Andover archives: John de Ponynton, John Erchebaud, Henry de Mourtone and John Oriold.[1] Nearly all of them are to be found in the records of the Andover Gild Merchant published by Gross in his second volume.[2] Thus in 1302, John Oriold was one of seven appointed by the forwardmen to revise the rules of the Gild, and in the following year he, John de Ponynton, Henry de Morton (later one of the Bailiffs), William Lucas and nine others were elected to a sub-committee *pro liberate saluanda*. In 1304, John Arnoue asked permission to transfer his second gild membership, acquired by inheritance, to his brother Walter. A collateral descendant may be the John Arnewe of Kimpton, whose wife Maud was, in 1430, allowed to escape from the custody of Richard Wyredrawer, town sergeant of Andover.[3]

Richard Lotyn was presumably related to the John Lotyn mentioned in 1314, a year in which the name of Richard de Marisco also occurs, while John Erchebaud appears in 1305 and 1328. In 1314 John de

1

Ponynton was deprived of his gild membership for bringing an action in the Court of King's Bench at Westminster against fellow Gildsmen, before attempting to decide the dispute in the gild's own court, contrary to its rules and his own oath.

Another quarrelsome gildsman (and possibly MP) was Roger de Clatford the Younger, who in 1303 received the membership previously held by Master John Asse. In 1322, Thomas Spirçok complained that Roger called him a great thief, alleging that he had taken and kept stray animals, and also that he had counterfeited the King's Seal. Roger denied the first two charges, and was instructed to find five compurgators to clear him of them on oath. He was unwilling to be tried on the third charge, and was therefore ordered to be distrained of his gild membership and declared "at mercy". Perhaps it was his father, rather than this apparently difficult individual, who represented Andover in the Parliament of 1306. John le Poer, possibly the MP of that name elected in 1307, sat on an inquisition relating to the Manor of Enham in 1292.[4]

Boroughs in the middle ages tended to regard representation in Parliament as a burden rather than a privilege. The members themselves were genuinely townsmen, as the names recorded above indicate, and not members of the gentry, as was increasingly the rule in later centuries, and, apart from the disruption of their business lives, they, no doubt, incurred some odium for agreeing to taxes which were then held to be binding on all. In addition the town was responsible for paying their expenses, which, at times, must have seemed disproportionate to any apparent benefit received. Unfortunately, the borough archives do not seem to throw any light on the costs incurred by Andover during these years, but the Gild records for 1338 show that John de Wyld and Adam Spircok received 22s for their expenses after a week's visit to London in connection with a law suit in Chancery.[5] It is possibly significant that no returns were made to the writs summoning Parliament to Lincoln in 1301, and although Andover members attended, first at Carlisle and then at Northampton in 1307, the additional burden imposed by the greatly increased distance from the town may have persuaded the thrifty burgesses to ignore the writs issued in 1309 and 1311, and the right to representation was evidently held to have lapsed thereafter.

Notes:

1   A.A. 1/31.
2   Gross, C., *The Gild Merchant*,II, 297-9, 307-9, 316, 324, 342.
3   Woodward, B. B., *A General History of Hampshire*, II, 350n.
4   *Chancery Inquisitions Post Mortem*, 20 Edward I, no. 14.
5   Gross, op. cit., II, 333.

Andover remained unrepresented in Parliament until 1586. By that time the situation had changed considerably. The gentry, no longer satisfied with the two seats available to them as Knights of the Shire, were invading the boroughs, and finding little difficulty in persuading the townsmen to elect them, free of expense, instead of bearing this financial burden themselves. The existing boroughs proved inadequate to meet their demands and in Elizabeth's reign alone 31 boroughs, with 62 members, were created or restored. Andover was the last of these.[1]

The restoration of the right to representation seems to have come through the influence of the Queen's favourite, the Earl of Leicester, then High Steward of the borough. In 1584, he wrote to the bailiffs and others:[2]

"After my heartie commendations. Whereas it has pleased her Majesty to appoint a Parliament to be presently called: being steward of your towne, I make bould heartily to pray you that you would give me the nomination of one of your burgesses for the same; and yf, minding to avoid the charges of allowance for the other burgesse, you mean to name any that is not of your town, if you will bestow the nomination of the other burgesse also on me, I will thank you for it; and will appoint a sufficient man, and see you discharged of all charges in that behalfe. And so praying your speedy answer herein, I thus bid you right heartilie farewell. From the Court, the 12th October 1584.

Your loving friend
R. LEYCESTER

If you will send me your election (return) with a blank, I will put in the names.
(Addressed) To my very loving friends, the bailiffs and the rest of the towne of Andover."

As High Steward, Leicester should no doubt have been aware that Andover had long ceased to return members, but as he was also

Robert Dudley, Earl of Leicester.   *1575 (Artist unknown)*

Steward of Great Yarmouth, King's Lynn, Bristol and Reading,[3] his confusion is perhaps pardonable. At any rate he seems to have lost no time in remedying the situation, and though he was too late for the Parliament of 1584, two years later Andover again sent two MP's to Westminster, after an interval of 279 years.

The inclusion of Andover made up the tally of Hampshire representatives in the unreformed Parliament where, in addition to the two County members, it joined Christchurch, Lymington, Petersfield, Portsmouth, Southampton, Stockbridge, Whitchurch, Winchester and three boroughs in the Isle of Wight.

Leicester did not live long enough to gain much from Andover's enfranchisement as he died on 4th September 1588, too early, presumably, to exercise any influence over the Parliament of 1589. In 1586, however, Sir John Neale considers it "doubtless" that "the Earl nominated both members" for Andover[4], but Leicester was in the Netherlands in 1586 and it is probable that at least some influence over the borough was exercised by Lord Sandys of the Vyne, who was a freeholder in the town, and possibly also by William West, first Lord Delaware, whose widow married a townsman. Edwin Sandys, one of the two members, presumably owed his election to the influence of Lord Sandys, who became his father-in-law five months before the opening of the 1586 Parliament; the two families having been previously unrelated. He was the nephew of the Archbishop of York of the same name, and a member of the Middle Temple. He later followed a military career and was knighted in Ireland in 1599.[5] His father became MP for Andover in 1593.

The name of the other member in 1586 appears in the official returns as James Halley, which seemed to indicate a possible local connection, since a "Wyllam Hallye G[entleman]" occurs among the "Free Suters of the Titheynge of the pryerye" in a list of residents in Andover between the ages of 12 and 70 drawn up in 1582.[6] However, he has recently been identified as James Hawley of Burston, near Brentford, Middlesex. His name was inserted in a different hand from that in the rest of the returns, which indicates that a blank was left to be filled in by Leicester. However, there is no known connection between him and the Earl, except possibly through intermediaries. Like Sandys a member of the Middle Temple, he died in 1608.[7]

6

Henry Reade, who was elected in 1589, bore a name which had a variety of connections with Hampshire. Sir Richard Rede (1511-1579), of Nether Wallop, became Master of Requests,[8] and there were Reades who flourished at Tangley in the reign of Elizabeth I.[9] The MP of 1589 was the second of the four sons of Anthony Reade, who purchased the manor of Faccombe in 1583. Henry Reade died in 1647, and both he and his wife Anne are commemorated in Faccombe Church. She was the daughter of Sir Thomas Windebank, Clerk of the Signet to Elizabeth and James I, and of Frances Dymoke, the daughter of the Queen's Champion Sir Edward Dymoke. Her sister Mildred married Henry Reade's younger brother Robert (of Linkenholt), whose second son, another Robert, was for a time secretary to his uncle Sir Francis Windebank (1582-1646), Secretary of State under Charles I; he is mentioned below in connection with Sir Thomas Jervoise and Sir Henry Rainsford, MP for Andover in 1640.[10] He seems to have owed both his seat in Parliament and his admission into the Middle Temple to Miles Sandys, the father of Edwin.[11]

Thomas Temple, the other MP elected in 1589, was the first Baronet of the Temples of Stowe (created in 1611). Educated at Oxford and Lincoln's Inn, he succeeded his father in 1603 and was knighted the same year. He was successively Sheriff of Oxford, Buckinghamshire and Warwickshire. About 1595 he married Hester, daughter of Miles Sandys of Latimers, Master of the King's Bench Office, who became MP for Andover in 1593.[12]

Miles Sandys, the brother of the Archbishop of York, and father of Edwin who represented Andover in 1586, "sat in every Parliament from 1563 to 1597, but never twice in the same seat. His constituencies, in chronological order, were Taunton, Leicester, Bridport, Buckinghamshire (his second wife's county), Abingdon, Plymouth, Andover and Stockbridge". He probably owed his election at Plymouth in 1588 and at Abingdon in 1586 to Leicester, and this suggests that the Earl played some part also in the election of his son Edwin in 1586.[13] Lord Sandys of the Vyne was probably his patron in 1593.[14]

The other member elected in 1593, Edward Baker, was also a royal official who in 1586 acted as rapporteur at the trial of Mary Queen of Scots,[15] and in 1597 was one of the seven Commissioners appointed to investigate Sir Thomas Sherley's accounts.[16] He was educated at Winchester and New College, Oxford, and was later a lawyer in the service of Archbishop Whitgift. He fell under suspicion at the time of Essex's rebellion, but was defended by Richard Bancroft, the future Archbishop of Canterbury, in a letter to Robert Cecil. His patron in 1593 was possibly Lord Delaware. After representing three other constituencies, he died in 1602.[17]

The second member for Andover in 1597 was Edward Reynolds, the Secretary of the Earl of Essex. At the time of the election Essex himself was taking part in the Islands Voyage, and during his absence it was probably Reynolds, later to be involved in his master's downfall, who organised the electoral campaign to gain supporters in the House of Commons. Essex, like his step-father, Leicester, was probably High Steward of Andover.[18]

The other member, Edward Phillips, or Phelips, the builder of Montacute, was MP for Somerset in 1601 and 1604 and Speaker in the first Parliament of James I's reign. He was by profession a barrister, another member of the Middle Temple, who became Serjeant at Law in 1603 and Master of the Rolls in 1611. He died in 1614.[19]

Another lawyer, Nicholas Hyde, also a member of the Middle Temple, represented the borough in 1601. His family came from Tisbury in Wiltshire, and he was born in Wardour Castle, but he had closer local connections, having married Margaret, daughter of Sir Arthur Swayne of Sarson, Amport. Elected for Christchurch in 1604 and for Bath in 1614 and 1625, he died in 1631. At first he was critical of royal policy, but changed his tune in 1626 and was made Lord Chief Justice of England after the death of Sir Ranulf Crew. His chief claim to fame, however, is probably that he was the uncle of the historian Edward Hyde, Earl of Clarendon.[20]

His fellow member was yet another barrister and Middle Templer, namely Henry Ludlow (1577-1639) of Hill Deverill and Tadley, Hampshire, the son-in-law of Lord Delaware; he was the uncle of Edmund Ludlow, the future regicide.[21] His younger half-brother, also called Henry, married Elizabeth Phelips or Phillips, the niece of Edward Phelips of Montacute - another example of family interconnections, as this would establish a relationship with

8

Sir Thomas Jermyn, of Rushbrook, Suffolk (1573-1645), MP in 1604, held a series of offices at Court, and was ultimately Comptroller of the Household and a Privy Councillor. Andover was his first parliamentary seat, and he subsequently sat for Suffolk in 1614 and for Bury St Edmunds from 1621-1628, as well as in the Short and Long Parliaments. In the latter assemblies, he attended as a spokesman for the King, but although disabled in 1644, he trimmed his sails sufficiently to avoid being declared a delinquent.[23]

Thomas Antrobus, the other MP elected in 1604, who died in 1622, was descended from a Cheshire family, but his father, described as "of London" was probably a merchant, and his mother, Elizabeth Woodcock, was the daughter of an Alderman. He was himself a lawyer, educated at Lincoln's Inn, and married Elizabeth, daughter of Sir Richard Norton of Rothersfield. He acquired the manor of Easton, north-east of Winchester, in 1605 from Sir Philip Sidney's daughter, Elizabeth, Countess of Rutland, and in 1608 bought Heath House, Petersfield.[24]

These early Andover MP's appear to have been elected for the most part as a result of Court influence or pressure from the local gentry. Leicester, as High Steward, was the first of these patrons, and Essex, who features in an eighteenth century list of High Stewards, was obviously able to nominate to membership. The Earl of Southampton, a supporter of Essex in the rising of 1601, filled this office a little later, since the town "payd our hy Steward the Lord of Southampton the 8 of October 1606 at the hart iii £."[25] Lord Sandys of the Vyne, another Essex supporter, who certainly nominated Miles Sandys as MP for Stockbridge in 1597, is also a possible patron.[26] In 1614, however, the bailiffs and approved men decided to show their independence by electing two of their own body. This is the more significant since 1614 was the year of the Addled Parliament, summoned by James I on the advice of one faction at Court called the "undertakers" because they promised to produce a tractable assembly - an aim which they conspicuously failed to achieve. It is probably not accidental that the official returns give the two townsmen the designation of "gent", unlike nearly all their predecessors who are assigned to the superior category of Esquire.

The two men in question were Richard Venables and Peter Noyes, and both had already filled the office of bailiff, the former in 1604-5 and the latter in 1602-3.[27] Venables' father, another Richard, died in 1598 leaving £100 to the poor, a gift commemorated on a board erected in Andover Church by his son.[28] In 1606 he himself was involved in a dispute with Lord Saye and Sele over the reversion of the parsonage at Andover, of which Venables was tenant. Lord Saye approached both Lord Salisbury and James I in an attempt to bring pressure on Winchester College, the patron of the living, maintaining that it should prefer "the lineal heir of the founder ... unto a Fellow both of small deservings and whose father but by marriage came to be tenant to the College, and yet since that time, partly by that and otherwise has clearly gained to the value of 3000*l*. at the least."[29] He was, evidently, a man prepared to defend himself against social pressures and sent to Lord Salisbury what appears to have been a successful petition safeguarding his rights. Peter Noyes was the son of Robert, bailiff 1577-8, who is listed among the freeholders of Hatherdeane in 1582, and in 1586 had lands assessed at £10 13s 4d. The two MP's were, with Richard Kemis, overseers of the will of Alexander Twitchin, first Headmaster of Andover Grammar School, who died in 1611.[30]

Richard Venables was re-elected in 1621 and with him the Steward of Andover, John Sutor or Shuter, a lawyer who represented the borough in later Parliaments, i.e. 1624, 1625 and 1626.[31] On the death of Venables, however, a by-election held in November 1621 led to his replacement by Robert Wallop of Farleigh Wallop, whose career is more appropriately considered in relation to the Long Parliament of 1640. A member of the Wallop family was elected to every Parliament between 1621 and 1640 except that of 1626, and this connection with Andover continued into the eighteenth century. In 1625 and 1626 Robert Wallop sat as Knight of the Shire for Hampshire, and in 1625 it was his father, Sir Henry (1568 - 1642), who represented Andover. He had already in 1597 sat for Lymington, in 1624 for Whitchurch, and in 1601 and 1621 for Hampshire, which he was to represent again in 1626, 1628 and the two Parliaments of 1640. He was then opposed to the Court and petitioned against Strafford's Irish administration. He was said to be "one of the wealthiest commoners of his day".[32] On 13th October 1625, Andover paid five shillings for the "museck att Scir harry Wallop feaste".[33]

Lord Henry Paulet, of Amport, MP in 1626, was the younger brother of the fourth Marquess of Winchester, famous for his defence of Basing House in the Civil War, and father of Francis Paulet who was elected for Andover in 1679 and 1681. Lord Henry married Lucy, daughter of Sir George Philpot of Thruxton, whose brothers Henry and Thomas were in 1646 suspected of being Popish recusants, and he may, like his elder brother, have been a Catholic himself. If so, this would explain why he represented Andover on one brief occasion only.[34]

In 1628 Ralph Conway was elected with Robert Wallop and this represents a reassertion of outside influences. Conway's father was Secretary of State and on 2nd February 1628 he wrote to Sir Thomas Jervoise, of Herriard, as he was "in some distress where to provide a burgess' place for his son Ralph. Understanding the power Sir Thomas has at Andover and in some places in Shropshire, earnestly requests that he would accommodate him in one of these places". Less than a fortnight later he wrote again to say that Sir Thomas "has made the Secretary's son his servant by procuring him access to that great Council, and giving him a sight of business and affairs. Desires to know what is to be done with regard to the 'customary feast' at the election, and whether it be requisite his son should be there at that time".[35]

Sir Thomas Jervoise (1587 - 1654), whose influence in Andover was thus emphatically demonstrated, was a Shropshire landowner descended from a London alderman, a mercer, and married to a Hampshire heiress, Lucy Powlett. He was seven times MP for Whitchurch and in 1640 Francis Read wrote to his cousin Robert: "Sir Thomas Jervoyse hath, as last time, engrossed both the burgess places of Whitchurch, that town being, I know not why, so much at his command that they dare not deny him".[36] Sir Thomas filled various local offices under the Crown but was, however, a Puritan, a cousin by marriage of the Wallops, and served in the Parliamentary Army against Charles I, besides being a member of the Committee for Hampshire.[37] In 1627 he presented to the living of Upper Clatford,[38] and his connection with Andover is also reflected in the town Chamber Accounts which show payments in 1627 for "Riding to Scir tho: Jearvoys", and in 1642 for "rideing 5 iourneys to Sr Thomas Jarvis".[39]

11

Notes:

1   Neale, J. E., *The Elizabethan House of Commons*, 141, 146.
2   Merewether, H. A., and Stephens, A. J., *The History of the Boroughs and Municipal Corporations of the United Kingdom*, II, 1593-4.
3   Neale, op. cit., 210.
4   Ibid., 211.
5   Hasler, P. W., *The House of Commons* 1558 - 1603, III, 339.
6   Bennett, A. C., and Parsons, E., *A History of the Free School of Andover*, 213.
7   Hasler, op. cit., I, 168; II, 282.
8   *D.N.B.* sub Rede, Sir Richard.
9.   Woodward, op. cit., III, 172n.
10   *V.C.H. Hants*, IV, 318; *D.N.B.* sub Read or Reade, Thomas, and Windebank, Sir Francis.
11   Hasler, op. cit., 168.
12   Cokayne, G. E., *The Complete Baronetage*, I, 82.
13   Neale, op. cit., 312, 179, 211.
14   Hasler, op. cit., III 339.
15   Read, C., *Lord Burghley and Queen Elizabeth*, 352.
16   H.M.C., *Salisbury*, VII, 368.
17   Hasler, op. cit., I, 392-3.
18   Neale, op. cit., 239; A.A. 1/76/-.
19   *D.N.B.* sub Phelips, Sir Edward; Dasent, A. J., *The Speakers of the House of Commons*, 382-3.
20   *D.N.B.*, sub Hyde, Nicholas; Hasler, op. cit., II, 364.
21   *The Wiltshire Archaeological Magazine* XXVI, 173; Hasler, op. cit., I, 168; II, 498.
22   *D.N.B.* sub Ludlow, Edmund; Keeler, M. F., *The Long Parliament, 1640 - 1641*, 260.
23   Keeler, op. cit., 234-5.
24   *V.C.H., Hants*, III, 118, 318; *Harleian Society*, XXII, 124.
25   A.A., 1/76/-; 1/23/3 p.3.
26   H.M.C., *Salisbury*, VII, 432.
27   Register ..., 2-3.
28   Bennett and Parsons, op. cit., 187.
29   H.M.C., *Salisbury*, XVIII, 266, 442; XIX, 501-2;, *C.S.P.Dom, Addenda, 1580 - 1625*, 471-2.

30   Davey, C. R., (ed.), *The Hampshire Lay Subsidy Rolls, 1586;*
      Bennett and Parsons, op. cit., 93, 185, 216;
31   Register ...2-3.
32   Keeler, op. cit., 376-8.
33   A.A., Chamber Accounts, 1/23/3, p.25.
34   *Burke's Peerage*, sub Winchester, Marquess of; Calendar of the
      Proceedings of the Committee for Compounding, II, 1082.
35   *C.S.P. Dom.*, 1627 - 1628, 541, 566.
36   *C.S.P. Dom.*, 1640 - 1641, 179.
37   Keeler, op. cit., 236-7.
38   *V.C.H., Hants,* IV, 365.
39   A.A. 1/23/3, p.33; 1/23/6, p.6.

Charles I's attempt to rule without Parliament ended in failure, after 11 years, in 1640. For the Short Parliament Andover elected a courtier, and an opponent of the King, in the persons of Sir Richard Wynn and Robert Wallop respectively. Wynn (1588 - 1649) was the second baronet of Gwydir whose father, Sir John, had died in 1627. He went to Court under the auspices of the Earl of Suffolk and on the fall of the Lord Treasurer found a new patron in the Earl of Pembroke. He was Gentleman of the Privy Chamber to Charles, when Prince of Wales, and assisted at his coronation. Knighted in 1616, he held a number of official positions including membership of the Council of Wales. He served in Parliament for Caernarvonshire in 1614 and for Ilchester between 1621 and 1625, and in the Long Parliament he was to represent Liverpool. He was one of the royal nominees for the Short Parliament and was returned for Newton and Bodmin, as well as Andover. Nevertheless, although suspended from the Long Parliament in 1642, he served the times so aptly that he was able to regain his place and died a member in 1649.[1]

Robert Wallop, who represented Andover in both the Parliaments of 1640, the second of them with Sir Henry Rainsford, had been an MP since 1621, mostly as a member for the borough, though he sat for the County in 1625 and 1626. During the Civil War period he showed himself, like his father Henry, a strong supporter of the parliamentary side, becoming a member of the Committee of Both Kingdoms in 1644 and sitting as one of Charles I's judges, though he did not actually sign his death warrant. His political outlook had by that time become Republican and he played a prominent part during the Interregnum, associating closely with Sir Henry Vane the Younger. In 1660 he was elected MP for Whitchurch but as a regicide was discharged from Parliament and "made incapable of bearing any office or place of public trust", and with some others was later condemned to be "drawn from the Tower of London upon sledges and hurdles, through the streets and highways, to and under the gallows at Tyburn, with ropes around their necks". He died in the Tower in 1667.[2]

Wallop's political views, no doubt, developed during the Civil War period but it must already have been clear in 1640 that he was a strong critic of the King. The burgesses of Andover, therefore, decided to play safe by selecting as their other member one who would be more favourable to the Court. On 26th October 1640, Francis Read wrote to his cousin Robert: "The town of Andover has most unexpectedly bestowed a place on Sir Henry Rainsford without any thought or suit of his, or, for aught I know, any of his friends. I am very glad of it, both because it comes as a healing plaster to divert his grief (caused by the death of his wife) and, by this means I have one friend more of the House than I thought".[3] The significance of Rainsford's election is underlined by the fact that out of 28 MP's elected for Hampshire in 1640, only eight were not parliamentarian in sympathy.[4]

Sir Henry Rainsford (1599 - 1641) was a landowner with property in Gloucestershire and at Combe, Hampshire. He had moved in literary circles as a young man and was later a friend of Lord Falkland, whose political views he seems to have shared; his son was certainly a Royalist. He served on several Committees in the Long Parliament but contracted smallpox in March 1641 and was dead by the end of the month, for on 31st March the House of Commons issued orders for a new writ to elect a replacement.[5]

The ensuing by-election was disputed but Rainsford's place was at first taken by Henry Vernon, probably of Hodnet, Shropshire, a first cousin of Thomas, fourth Earl of Southampton. In April he voted against the attainder of Charles I's fallen minister Strafford, and in the Civil War he was, predictably, a Royalist.[6] It is, therefore, at first sight surprising that he should have been commended to the electors of Andover by Robert Wallop, who wrote to the bailiff on 31st March 1641: "It hath pleased God lately to take away Sir Henry Rainsford; for the supplyinge of whose place this gentleman Mr. Henry Vernon now makes his addresse unto you. His worth and abilities will sufficiently commend themselves, yett if you please to afford him yr favourable respect by reason of my recommendation, I shall both for this and your former favours bee ever ready to acknowledge myselfe to bee your very lovinge friend & Servant".[7]

The explanation of this unexpected canvassing was probably family relationship: Wallop had married Anne, the Earl of Southampton's sister, who was also Vernon's cousin.[8]

Vernon's stay in the House of Commons was in any case a short one for

Sir William Waller, who had been declared the defeated candidate, submitted a petition on 30th April, after which Vernon was probably disabled from sitting until the case had been decided.[9] It was not till 3rd May 1642 that a report was made to the House on "the State of the Election for Andevor":

"There are in the Town Twenty four Burgesses, that have Right of Election: That Eighteen only appeared, and that Nine were for Mr. Vernon, and Nine for Sir Wm. Waller: That the Bailiff, who challenges a casting voice, gave his voice for Mr. Vernon; and returned him: That there was One Mr. Bourne, who was elected, but not sworn, that was there at the Door; but could not be admitted during the Time of the Election: The Election being done, he came to the Bailiff, and said, that he was there to give his Voice to Sir Wm. Waller: The Bailiff answered him, That he had no voice here; being only elected a Burgess, and not sworn. There were Two other Burgesses, Wm. Barwick, and another, that were at the Town-hall before the Election began; but they were all generally put out, as not being sworn: But they came not to give their Voice, during the time of the Election, as the other did; but, after the Election ended, then they came, and said that they were come to give their Voices for Mr. Vernon".[10]

Bourne and Barwick seem to have left no traces in the Andover records, and the name of the third burgess mentioned cannot even be conjectured. It seems likely that both sides were making every effort to gain a majority, and possibly the appointments of all three were temporary.[11] At any rate, the House divided on party lines as the continuation of the Journal indicates:

"Resolved, upon the Question, That Mr. Vernon's Election to serve as a Burgess in this Parliament, for the Town of Andevor, is void; The Question being proposed, Whether Sir Wm. Waller's Election be good;

The House was divided.
The Yeas went forth.

16

Sir Philip Stapilton	)	Tellers for the Yea - 107
Mr. Jo Moore	)	
Mr. Kirton	)	Tellers for the Noe - 102
Sir Edward Alford	)	

Resolved, upon the Question, That Election of Sir Wm. Waller, for a Burgess of the Town of Andevor, is a good Election: And that the Bailiff of the said Town do, at the Bar, amend the Return."

The Tellers in the division were two parliamentarians for the Yeas and two royalists for the Noes.[12]

The decision of the House was implemented on 12th May:

"The Bailiff of Andevor, who had formerly returned Mr. Vernon to serve for Andevor, whose Election is since judged void was, by order, summoned to appear here; And did this Day appear here, with the Clerk of the Crown, to amend the Indenture of the Return; And did, at the Bar, amend it accordingly; and made it for Sir Wm. Waller".[13]

Waller was the son of Sir Thomas Waller, Lieutenant of Dover Castle, and after serving abroad as a young man in the Thirty Years' War, he married a west country heiress. He supported Parliament from the beginning of the Civil War, being largely instrumental in the capture of Portsmouth. Later successes, including the capture in September 1642 of Winchester Castle, of which he had formerly been Governor, earned him the nickname of "William the Conqueror", but he received a check at Roundway Down, and in spite of later victories at Alton and Cheriton, he was included in the number of those who surrendered their commissions under the Self-Denying Ordinance. In October 1644, he had been surprised by the Royalists at Andover. "It was a great mercy of God", he wrote later, "that when the King came suddenly upon me with his whole Army att Andover and I had then nothing but a mere body of horse and dragoons with me, I made a fair retreat to Basingstoke."

Sir William Waller (after Cornellius Jonson)

Waller had been elected to the Committee of Public Safety after only eight weeks in Parliament, and continued to serve on the Committee of Both Kingdoms after giving up his military command until the end of 1645. As a member of the Committee for Hampshire he witnessed the capture of Basing House by Cromwell. He became one of the leaders of the "Presbyterian" party in Parliament and as such was disabled from sitting on 14th March 1647, when it was "Ordered, That a warrant shall issue forth, under Mr. Speaker's Hand, directed to the Clerk of the Crown in Chancery, to issue forth a Writ, for the new Election of a Burgess to serve in this present Parliament for the Town of Andover in the County of Southampton in the place of Sir Wm. Waller formerly elected to serve in that Place, but since disabled."[14]

This order was revoked on 8th June 1648,[15] but Waller was

subsequently again excluded at the time of Pride's Purge, and was imprisoned by the Army for three years. When the Long Parliament was restored by Monk early in 1660 he resumed his seat, but though he supported the Restoration, he played no further part in the national life, dying in 1668.[16]

An incident recorded in his "Experiences" which refers to his constituency may perhaps be included here:

> "When I took the Lord Piercy att Andover, having att that time an inconvenient distemper, I desired Collonell Cromwell to entertaine him with some civility; who did afterwards tell me, that amongst those whom we tooke with him (being about thirty) their was a youth of so faire a countenance, that he doubted of his condition; and to confirm himself willed him to sing; which he did with such a daintiness that Cromwell scrupled not to say to Lord Piercy; that being a warriour, he did wisely to be accompanied by Amazons; on which that Lord, in some confusion, did acknowledge that she was a damsel; this afterwards gave cause for scoff at the King's party, as that they were loose and wanton, and minded their pleasure more than either their Country's service or their Maister's good".[17]

During the Interregnum Andover was to a large extent disfranchised. No representatives appear to have sat in Barebones Parliament in 1653, and although John Dunck, or Dunch, was returned for the first Parliament of the Protectorate in 1654, he chose to sit for Berkshire. The Commons ordered "That a Warrant issue forth under Mr. Speaker's Hand, directed to the Clerk of the Commonwealth, for a new Writ for electing of another Burgess for the Town of Andever in the Stead of Mr. Dunk",[18] but no action appears to have been taken.

The records of Andover show that there were two other candidates, the Recorder John Shuter, four times MP during the 1620's, who was declared elected but does not appear on the official return, and John Bulkley, at the bottom of the poll with seven votes. On the same day, 6th July 1654, Richard Cromwell, the Protector's son and eventual heir, was unanimously chosen High Steward of Andover.[19]

John Dunch, who died in 1668, was the only son of Samuel Dunch of

19

Richard Cromwell (artist unknown)

North Baddesley, and Dulcibella, daughter of John More, Serjeant at Law, who was Steward of Andover from 1599 to 1620 and possibly earlier. He married Ann, daughter of Richard Major of Hursley, whose other daughter Dorothy married Richard Cromwell. His family was already connected with the Protector by the marriage of his uncle, Sir William Dunch, to Mary, daughter of Sir Henry Cromwell, who thus became Oliver's aunt by marriage. His cousin, Edmund Dunch, was a member of the Long Parliament for Wallingford and in 1658 was made Baron Burnell by Cromwell.[20]

A letter from the Protector to his "loving friend John Dunch Esquire", written on 27th August 1657, has survived: "I desire to speak with you; and hearing a report from Hursley that you was going to your Father's in Berkshire, I send this express to you, desiring you to come to me to Hampton Court".[21]

In a letter of the Council dated December 1657, Dunch is mentioned as the first of the Commissioners of the Peace for Hampshire,[22] and in June 1658 his name was added to the list of Commissioners for ejecting scandalous ministers in the county.[23] Dunch was one of those who voted in favour of Cromwell taking the title of King.[24]

No MP's for Andover were returned for the second Parliament of the Protectorate, though there were two members for the brief session under Richard Cromwell in 1659. One of these, Robert Gough, of Vernham's Deane, may have been related to the regicide William Gough (or Goffe), the Major-General in charge of Hampshire, Sussex and Berkshire, who died in 1679 and was called by Ludlow a creature of Richard Cromwell.[25] The other, Gabriel Beck, of Westminster, was Solicitor of the Council of State during the Commonwealth and married Ann, the sister of John Dunch.[26]

Notes:

1	Keeler, op. cit., 402-3; Cokayne, *Complete Baronetage*, I, 64.
2	*D.N.B.* Sub Wallop, Robert.
3	*C.S.P. Dom., 1640 - 1641*, 198.
4	Keeler, op. cit., 48.
5	ibid., 373-4.

6   ibid., 373-4.

7   A.A., 1/3/-

8   Keeler, op. cit., 374.

9   ibid, loc cit.

10   *H.C.J.*, II, 554.

11   Register ..., 5.

12   Keeler, op. cit., 49.

13   *H.C.J.*, II, 568.

14   ibid, VII, 497.

15   ibid, VII, 589.

16   *D.N.B.* sub Waller, Sir William; Adair, J., *Roundhead General*, 41, 51, 168, 189.

17   Adair, op. cit., 186.

18   *H.C.J.*, III, 373.

19   A.A. 1/2/42.

20   Woodward, op. cit., I, 369, 321; II, 110; V.C.H., Hants, II, 464; Noble, M., *Memoirs of the Protectoral House of Cromwell*, II, 442-3.

21   Abbott, W. C., *The Writings and Speeches of Oliver Cromwell*, IV, 613.

22   ibid, 689.

23   *C.S.P. Dom.*, 1658 - 1659, 42.

24   Keeler, op. cit. 161-2.

25   *D.N.B.* sub Goffe (or Gough), William; Ashley, M., *Cromwell's Generals*, 156.

26   Noble, op. cit., II, 443; *C.S.P. Dom., 1658 - 1659*, 95, 233.

The Andover members of the Convention, which negotiated Charles II's Restoration, were re-elected to the Cavalier Parliament a year later, and were both local men. Sir John Trott (c1615 - 1672) was the son of a London merchant who bought the family seat of Ash, Laverstoke, from Thomas Wills, Clerk of the Crown in Chancery, in 1649.[1] He himself married Elizabeth, daughter of Sir Edmund Wright, who was Lord Mayor of London in 1640. He was Sheriff of Hampshire in 1651, and in 1650 put forward a claim to the sequestrated Manor of Upclatford, the property of Richard Atkins and Lady Acheson his wife.   In spite of his background as a Presbyterian and former supporter of the Commonwealth, he was made a baronet in October 1660, soon after the Restoration, and represented Andover in Parliament until his death. He is thought to have been guyed by Sir George Etherege in his *Man of Mode*, where he allegedly features as an awkward Hampshire footman.[2]

John Collins of Chute Lodge, Wiltshire, the other member elected in 1660, was an Anglican and committed royalist - a further example of the Andover burgesses hedging their bets. He was educated at Eton, King's College, Cambridge and Gray's Inn, eventually becoming Steward of the College. He represented Andover in four Parliaments but was not a very active member, though he was on the committee to enable Lord Henry Powlett to sell the Manor of Abbotts Ann. He was Steward of Andover from 1660 to 1679 when the Country Party which opposed Charles II gained control of the borough. He was succeeded as Steward at first by William Wither and then by William Guidott, but some of the Corporation protested that the election had been rigged. The Privy Council ordered a new bailiff to be sworn in and Collins regained the Stewardship. At the same time the Whig members of the corporation were replaced. Collins was knighted for his services to the Court, but after the Revolution of 1688 he apparently became a non-juror and lost his estate.[3]

Sir John Trott's death led to a by-election in January 1673, in which Sir Kingsmill Lucy (c1649 - 1678) was returned. He was "re-elected after Lord Chancellor Shaftesbury's writs had been declared void by the House of Commons. He made his mark by an attack on Lauderdale, but later went over to the Court". He was the second baronet, the son of Sir Richard and great-grandson of Sir Thomas Lucy of Charlecote, the putative original of Shakespeare's Justice Shallow, and had property at Faccombe and Netley, Hampshire. He was educated at Lincoln's Inn, and married the daughter of the first Earl of Berkeley.[4]

Lucy died before the end of what has been called "the Long Parliament of Charles II's reign", and a by-election in 1678 led to the return of the Hon. Charles West, the eldest son of the fifth Lord de la Warr (1626 - 1687), whose property at Wherwell Priory explains his influence in the borough. West, who was again elected at Andover in 1681, predeceased his father.[5] The by-election of 1678 was disputed and led to an unsuccessful petition by the defeated candidate John Dean.[6]

In 1679, Francis Paulet, the grandfather of the twelfth Marquess of Winchester, who was to represent Andover in 1680, 1689 and 1690, was returned for the first time. He was the son of Lord Henry Paulet, MP in 1626, but had shed the Catholic leanings of his family and his election was a setback for the Court. So too was that of his fellow member, the Steward of Andover, William Wither of Manydown, Lawrence Wootton, Hampshire (1648 - 1679), who came of a family with strong Roundhead associations. His father was described by Richard Cromwell as "an active man, and one that Wallop hath disobleiged", while he himself was assistant to Lord Fauconberg, the husband of Cromwell's daughter, Mary, during his embassy to Venice.[7] His election was the occasion of an unsuccessful petition from John Pollen (MP 1690) "complaining that William Withers Esquire combining with the Bailiff of the Borough of Andover in the County of Southampton did, by several illegal and unwarrantable practices, procure himself to be returned to serve in this present Parliament".[8] In 1680 the election of Sir Robert Henley of the Grange, near Alresford, whose son Anthony was MP 1698 - 1700, was also probably a defeat for the Court.[9] In 1681, however, the election of Charles West and John Collins for the Oxford Parliament reflected a reaction in favour of Charles II. The defeated candidates petitioned, without success, on the grounds that the franchise should be extended to the freemen of the borough in general.[10]

The Andover representatives in James II's Parliament, Collins and Colonel Robert Phillips, were both supporters of the Court. A claim for an extended franchise was thwarted by Robinson, the sub steward

24

or town clerk, who threatened to prosecute the claimants for riot.[11] As a result he was removed from office in 1688. Phillips was the second son of Sir Robert Phillips (or Phelips) (1586 - 1638), a Parliamentarian, but was himself a Colonel in the king's army.[12] He helped Charles II in his escape after the Battle of Worcester, was arrested, imprisoned in the Tower, but escaped and joined the King in exile. MP for Stockbridge in 1660, he was made Groom of the Bedchamber by Charles II and Chancellor of the Duchy of Lancaster by James II, but lost his office soon after the Revolution.[13]

In 1688 James II contemplated calling another Parliament in order to repeal the laws against Catholics, and carried out a nation-wide canvass among JP's and other prominent individuals. These enquiries shed light on the views of some of the Andover MP's mentioned above. Sir John Collins of Chute Lodge, a Deputy Lieutenant of Wiltshire, gave entirely satisfactory answers:

> "1.   Declares his judgement is for taking of(f) the penal laws and tests.
> 2.   He will contribute to the election of such members as shall do it.
> 3.   He will live friendly and peaceably with persons of all persuasions."

Under the heading "Whitchurch", it was noted that "If Sir John Collins loose his interest in Andover, he may be supported here, perhaps with success".

Francis Paulet, on the other hand, refused to answer the first two questions ("whether you will be for the taking of the Test and Penall Laws" and "Whether you will contribute all that lys in your power to chuse such Members, as will be for the taking of the Test and Penal laws"), but consented to the third ("Whether you will live friendly with your neighbours, whatsoever Religion they are of").

Under the heading "Andover" it was noted:

> "Has no Mayor, but only a Bayliff, whose place depends upon the King, and who makes a return of their members.

Sr John Collins	)	Served in the late Parliament
Robert Philips Esqr	)	
Gabriel Whistler Esqr	)	Designe to stand for the next,
Francis Paulet Esqr	)	and will neither comply

But t'is say'd the Town has invited Sr Robert Sawyer to stand in Sr John Collins his place.

This town will likewise require a thorough purge."

(Sawyer, of Highclere, had been Attorney General, Speaker of the House of Commons in 1678 and was to represent Cambridge University in the Convention Parliament).

After the report on Andover it is a little unexpected that James's agents in September 1688 reported of it: "Not yet settled but a good election expected".[14] The explanation may be that the corporation had come under Tory control in 1681 and had sent a loyal address on the dissolution of the Oxford Parliament. The Marquess of Winchester had then persuaded the corporation to surrender its Charter which had been replaced by a new and more favourable one, giving it control of the Weyhill Fair. After the expulsion of the Whigs the corporation had later "abhorred" the Rye House Plot against Charles II and had congratulated James II on his accession to the throne.[15]

The two Andover members of the Convention Parliament were on different sides. Francis Paulet had shown himself an opponent of James II, but the other member, John Pollen, the unsuccessful petitioner against William Wither in 1679 and MP again in 1690, was one of those who, on 5th February 1689, voted against granting William and Mary the title of King and Queen.[16] He was a member of a family which was prominent in Andover for two and a half centuries. His father Edward was a London merchant who died in 1636. Soon after, John Pollen married Anne, the widow of Nicholas Venables, the owner of the house known as the Priory. Pollen built almshouses and also endowed a school in his will (1718).[17]

A petition was presented on the opening day of the Convention by "Sir Robert Henley Knight and John Venables Esquire on behalf of themselves and the Body of the Burgesses of the Borough of Andover

26

in the County of Southampton, complaining of an undue Return, made by the Bailiff of the said Borough, of Burgesses to serve in this present Convention". It was, however, unsuccessful.[18]

This petition raised the question of where the right of election in Andover lay. There is no evidence concerning the medieval parliaments, but it is probable that the members of the Gild Merchant voted. When Andover's franchise was restored in 1586 the Charter of Elizabeth I's reign setting up the closed corporation had not yet been issued, but the returning officers were the bailiffs and it seems probable that only a limited number of the burgesses had the right to vote. The return of 1586 mentions the Corporation only, but those of 1588, 1597 and 1601 refer to "the consent of the corporacon and commonaltie".[19] Certainly once the corporation was closed only the Bailiff and select burgesses appear, on the evidence available, ever to have exercised the franchise, which was thus restricted to 24. This gave Andover one of the smallest electorates in the unreformed parliament, and in Hampshire, Lymington was the only other borough with equally few electors, while Southampton, at the opposite extreme, had three hundred.[20]

The election of 1689 was disputed and the report of the Committee of Privileges and Elections made on 1st April dealt with the question at considerable length and concluded that the right of election was "in the Bailiff and select Number of Burgesses only". Francis Paulet and John Pollen were, therefore, declared duly elected.*[21]

The recommendations of the Committee were accepted by the House and were regarded as decisive in future election disputes concerning the right to vote in Andover.

This restriction of the franchise was part of a general process affecting other constituencies. "Such existing tendencies were significantly enhanced by the last Determination Act of 1696, reinforced by the more notorious amending Act of 1729. These Acts purported to be 'for all the more effectual preventing of bribery and corruption in the election of members to serve in Parliament'. Their real intention was to lay down the principles for determining the legality of the franchise in a constituency. The Act of 1696 had laid it down that the most recent decision should stand. In 1729, however, an amendment declared

27

final and binding the previous, or last, determination 'all usages to be contrary notwithstanding'. In other words Parliament could for all time decide and determine the nature of the franchise in a constituency after a disputed return, whatever evidence existed.[22]

Notes:

1   *V.C.H., Hants, IV, 200.*
2   *Calendar of the Proceedings of the Committee for Compounding,* II, 1086; IV, 2697-8; Cockayne, *Complete Baronetage,* III, 195; Henning, B. D., *The House of Commons, 1660 - 1690,* III, 608; Woodward, op. cit., III, 246.
3   Register ..., 4-5; Henning, op. cit., I, 24-7; II, 107-8.
4   *Henning, op. cit., I, 246; II, 777;D.N.B,* sub Lucy, Sir Thomas; Cokayne, *Complete Baronetage,* I, 114.
5   *Burke's Peerage,* sub De la Warr.
6   *H.C.J.* IX, 533.
7   Wither, Rev. R. F. B., *The Wither Family,* 36; Register ... 6-7.
8   *H.C.J.* IX, 578.
9   D.N.B. sub Henley, Anthony.
10 Henning, op. cit., I, 245.
11 ibid, I, 245-7.
12 *D.N.B.* sub Phelips, Sir Robert.
13 Ollard, R., *The Escape of Charles II after the battle of Worcester,* 145.
14 Duckett, G., *Penal Laws and the Test Act,* I, 212, 422-3, 429-33..
15 Henning, op. cit., I, 245.
16 Feiling, I., *History of the Tory Party,* 497.
17 Earney, H. W., *Men of Andevor,* 10-11; Bennett and Parsons, op. cit., 8.
18 *H.C.J.* X, 10.
19 A.A., Shaw's Notebook E.
20 Speck, W. A., *Tory and Whig: the Struggle in the Constituencies, 1701 - 1715,* 129.
*   See Appendix B.
21 *H.C.J.,* X, 70-71.
22 O'Gorman, F., *Voters, Patrons and Parties: the Unreformed Electoral System of Hanoverian England, 1734 - 1832,* 12-13.

Attempts were made as early as the opening years of the Long Parliament to ensure that Parliaments were summoned regularly and at short intervals, but it was not till the passing of the Triennial Act in 1694 that the maximum life of Parliament was limited to three years, a restriction which lasted until the passing of the Septennial Act in 1715 extended it to seven. In the intervening period party feeling reached a position of bitterness which has rarely been equalled.

One of the Members for Andover elected in 1695 was Sir Robert Smyth, of Upton, the third baronet of his line (c1659 - 1745). Educated at the Middle Temple and St Alban Hall, Oxford, he married Anne Button of Libbington, Hampshire, widow of John Button of Buckland and daughter of Henry Whitehead of Titherley, whose wife Sarah was the daughter of Richard Norton of Southwick. He thus had strong Hampshire connections.[1]

The outstanding MP for Andover during the period of Triennial Parliaments was undoubtedly John Smith (1655 - 1723), of South Tidworth. After previously sitting for Ludgershall and Beeralston, he represented the borough from 1695 to 1713 and then from 1715 until his death was member for East Looe, Cornwall. He acted as Whip for the Whigs in the Convention Parliament, was a Lord of the Treasury from 1694 to 1699, and Chancellor of the Exchequer from 1699 till 1701.[2] In 1705 he was elected Speaker and this adds poignancy to an incident which occurred in January 1698. Smith became involved in an argument in the course of which he told the Speaker that "he should learn more manners", and threatened that, "if he treated him no better, he would pull him by the nose".[3]

In a description of Smith written at the beginning of Anne's reign, for the benefit of Sophia of Hanover and her son, he is called "a gentleman of good Estate in Hampshire ... of much Honour, a Lover of the Constitution of his Country; a very agreeable Companion in Conversation, a bold Orator in the House of Commons, when the interest of his Country is at Stake; of a good Address, Middle Stature, fair Complexion, turned of forty years old".[4]

Smith's election as Speaker in 1705 was one of the most controversial in the history of that high position. Burnet, a contemporary, described how "The Court declared for Mr. Smith ... he had from his first setting out in the world, been thoroughly in the principles and interests of the Whigs - yet with a due temper in all personal things, with relation to the Tories; but they all declared against him for Mr. Bromley, a man of grave deportment, and good morals, but looked upon as a violent Tory, and as a great favourer of Jacobites; which appeared evidently in a relation he printed of his travels".[5]

Smith was not, however, the first choice of Godolphin, the Lord Treasurer, who had previously approached Harley and Harcourt; but they both refused to stand. There were signs that the Whigs might back Bromley against the Court, whose candidate in 1701 had been defeated by Harley. Godolphin's choice of Smith was, therefore, designed to secure the support of the Whigs against the extreme Tories, or "Tackers", so called because they had "tacked" an Occasional Conformity Bill onto the Land Tax Bill in November 1704. As the Lord Treasurer told a meeting of "about 30 of the principal officers of the Crown" at the Chancellor of the Exchequer's, "there was a partye that nothing would satisfy but wresting the administration out of the Queen's hands ... he thought in such a conjunction they would not do the Queen or their country better service than in choosing Mr. Smith for the Speaker".

Harley, himself a Tory, concurred in Godolphin's choice but wrote that the Whigs "ought not to think they have imposed him upon the Court, but take it as a grace that they have him from the Queen's influence".

A week before the voting a contemporary noted: "The Election of the Speaker is still very uncertain, for at least twenty of Mr. Smith's friends are absent".[6]

The debate itself was described by the Marchioness of Granby in a letter to her father-in-law, the Duke of Rutland. Lord Granby, after praising Smith's "zeal for liberty and property, the present government, and the succession of the Crown in the Protestant line", moved that he should take the chair. "Then Sir John Holland seconded my Lord, after which my Lord Dysart proposed Mr. Bromley ... Then several spoke of both sides, but at last Mr. Smith

30

John Smith - Speaker of the House of Commons
(after Kneller)

carried it by 43, he having 249, and Mr. Bromley 206".[7]

In spite of pressure from the Court, no less than seventeen placemen voted against Smith, "among them George Clarke, most influential of private members and secretary to Prince George, who received the news of his dismissal then and there in the lobby, as he went to vote".[8] Eighty-one placemen voted for Smith; among his other supporters was Francis Shepheard, his fellow member for Andover, while Queen Anne presented him with a "purse of 1000 Guineas as a token of her satisfaction of his choice".[9]

While Speaker, Smith was one of the Commissioners for the Treaty of Union with Scotland, his signature following those of the Peers, and he thus became the first Speaker of Great Britain. In 1708, however, he stood aside in favour of Sir Richard Onslow, but was appointed Chancellor of the Exchequer again, holding that office from 1708 to 1710, and he was also one of the managers of the ill-fated impeachment of Dr. Sacheverell. Even after his retirement from the Government he remained one of the four principal Tellers of the Exchequer, a lucrative sinecure, and continued to hold this post even at the height of Tory power in 1712 and 1713, a fact which did not escape the notice of Toland, who, in his "Invitation to Dismal" (Lord Nottingham) wrote:

> "Wine can clear up Godolphin's cloudy face,
> And fill Jack Smith with hopes to keep his place."

The remainder of the ex-Speaker's political career was on the whole uneventful. He supported Walpole against Stanhope at the beginning of George I's reign, and opposed the Peerage Bill of 1719. His only son, Captain William Smith, died without issue, and the family property passed to a nephew, Thomas Assheton of Ashley, Cheshire, who assumed the name of Smith, and was the ancestor of two later Andover MP's, Thomas Assheton Smith, father and son.

Anthony Henley of The Grange, near Alresford, who was MP for Andover from 1698 to 1700, was the son of Sir Robert Henley, who as mentioned above was elected in 1679. Educated at Magdalen College, Oxford, he inherited £3,000 a year from his grandfather, who had been Master of the Court of King's Bench. Although a consistent Whig, and a member of the Kit Cat Club, he was also a friend of Swift.[10] When, in September 1699, the Andover Corporation discharged five burgesses for a variety of reasons, they felt it necessary to reassure Smith and Henley that this was done in order to "putt in more substantiall & discreet men in their roome thereby to make our Corporacon more reputable", and not to "lessen Your Interest"; on the contrary, "your manifold Kindness & favours to our Corporacon have layd such obligacons on Us that wee shall alwaies show Gratitude to you".[11]

Francis Shepheard, who supported Smith for the Speakership in 1705, was elected MP for Andover in 1701, 1702 and 1705. His father, Samuel Shepheard, was reckoned by contemporaries as "by far the first (trader) in England", and as "an excellent merchant for shipping and foreign trade". He was a vintner who at first traded in the Mediterranean before becoming a highly successful interloper in the Indian trade, and after the Revolution he had the largest single holding in the New (Whiggish) East India Company. He died in 1718 worth £800,000. He himself secured election in 1707 for Newport, Isle of Wight, while his other son, Samuel, held yet a third seat at Malmesbury. Governor Pitt, later the owner of Abbotts Ann, commented sarcastically on the parliament of 1701: "Certainly the sheep can never goe astray when they have so many Shepheards".

Their election was part of a widespread campaign on behalf of the New East India Company, which succeeded in securing the election of 67 MP's connected with it. It is possible that Anthony Henley, whose brother-in-law Janssen was a director of the Company, was persuaded to stand aside in favour of Francis Shepheard. John Smith also had shares in the New East India Company.

When Parliament met, however, the Tory Squires, led by Sir Edward Seymour, launched a counter-attack on the Whig carpet-baggers, and "the Shepheards were now subjected to an extended inquiry at the bar of the House, lasting over six sittings, at the end of which the elder Samuel was voted guilty of bribery in five constituencies and he and his two sons expelled from the House and sent to the Tower".[12]

In the course of these proceedings the Bailiff of Andover, Julius Samborne, and two burgesses, Joseph Wimbleton and Edward Warham, were ordered to be taken into the custody of the Serjeant at

Arms and were only released after acknowledging their faults in a petition, begging pardon and requesting to be discharged. They were then brought to the Bar of the House and reprimanded on their knees.[13] The Election Committee had meanwhile concluded that an endeavour had been made at Andover "corruptly to set to sale the election of a burgess"; and the House of Commons resolved "that the lending of money upon any security to a Corporation, and remitting the interest to influence the election of members to Parliament, is an unlawful and dangerous practice".[14]

Another disputed election occurred in the first Parliament of Anne's reign, when Smith and Shepheard were again returned. It was alleged that "The mobb or Populace then made a stirr & great noyse in the Streett headed by some Quakers and factious persons & chose (with their hands & seals fixed to an Indenture) Sir John Cope & Francis Conway Esq[r]".[15] Sir John Cope then presented a petition "asserting the undoubted right of the burgesses, freeholders and inhabitants, against the right of the bailiff and capital burgesses only ... it was complained also of the disfranchisement of some of the burgesses without any cause. On this petition no evidence being offered by the petitioners, the Committee resolved again, in conformity with the resolution of 1689, that the right was in 'the bailiff and select number of burgesses only'".[16]

Meanwhile, on 24th December 1702, William Bromley, the Chairman of the Committee of Privileges and Elections, had ordered "That the Bailiffe, approved men & Burgesses of Andover or some for them doe attend this Comtee ... with the Charters of Corporation granted to the said Borough & the Book commonly called the Manuloquium Book of & before the Reign of Queen Elizabeth".[17]

On 19th December, accordingly, the corporation instructed Mr. Barton, the Deputy Steward and Town Clerk, to "take care to drawe Records and to ffee Councel to defend the right of the present sitting Members", his expenses, and those of the Bailiff and any other members of the Corporation accompanying him to London, being paid by the Town Chamberlain.[18]

Sir John Cope (1673 - 1749), of Bramshill, one of the unsuccessful petitioners, became the sixth baronet, having already been knighted in the lifetime of his father. He served in four successive Parliaments in Anne's reign and was MP for Hampshire under George II.[19]

The other petitioner, Francis Seymour Conway (1679 - 1732), was the second son of Sir Edward Seymour Bt, Speaker of the House of Commons, who adopted the surname and arms of Conway on inheriting the property of his cousin, the last Earl of that name. He was himself raised to the peerage as Lord Conway in 1703.[20]

For most of Anne's reign the parliamentary patronage at Andover had been exercised by the Duke of Bolton (a title held by the Marquess of Winchester from 1689 to 1794) but the Tory predominance at the end of the reign led to his replacement by the Duke of Beaufort, who wrote to Harley in 1710 of how "everything has a good face here, and every face full of joy, to see themselves delivered from the management of the Duke of Bolton". About two years later Beaufort was made High Steward of Andover, and his influence was clearly strong in the election of 1713, when a High Tory was returned in the person of Sir Ambrose Crowley (1658 - 1713). Crowley's son John, MP for Okehampton 1722 - 1727, and for Queenborough 1727 - 1728, was arrested in 1715 on suspicion of being a Jacobite and offered the enormous sum of £100,000 bail (without success). The workers in the family business were also anti-Whiggish and remained Tories almost to the end of the century. Sir Ambrose himself, a Quaker by upbringing, was the owner of the Crowley Iron Works in Durham, probably the biggest in the country, and had a distinguished career in the City of London as Common Councillor, Sheriff and Alderman, being knighted in 1707. He was also a Deputy Governor of the East India Company. It has been conjectured that he lent the Duke of Beaufort a large sum and that his election at Andover was a reward for this service. His fellow MP in 1713, William Guidott, whose career is noted below, was an associate of one of Crowley's customers, Sir Henry Johnson.[21] The election result was contested by Governor Pitt (1653 - 1726), the unsuccessful candidate, but Crowley was dead before the petition could be heard.[22]

Gilbert Searle, who took Crowley's place in the by-election of 1714, may have been related to the George Searle, a member of a merchant family from Honiton, who was MP for Taunton in the Long Parliament. It was probably he who presented to the living of Eastrop,

Hampshire in 1699 and who was still alive eighteen years later. He died before 1732, leaving a son under age in the guardianship of his widow.[23]

Notes:

1   Cokayne, *Complete Baronetage*, IV, 10.

2   *D.N.B.* sub Smith, John.

3   *C.S.P., Dom., 1698,* 43.

4   Gray, J. M. (ed.) *Memoirs of the Life of Sir John Clerk,* 90-91.

5   Manning, J. A., *Lives of the Speakers of the House of Common* 409.

6   Speck, W. A., "The Choice of a Speaker in 1705", *Bulletin of the Institute of Historical Research,* XXXVII, no. 95, 20-46.

7   *H.M.C.,* Rutland, II, 183.

8   Feiling, op. cit., 389.

9   Hearne, *Remains,* I, 61, quoted in Morgan, W. T., *English Political Parties and Leaders in the Reign of Queen Anne,* 125.

10   *D.N.B.* sub Henley, Anthony.

11   Register ..., 8-9; *The Corporation of Andover, 1599 - 1835* (Andover Local Archives no. 4), ed. Darral and Spaul, 10.

12   Walcote, R., "The East India Interest in the General Election of 1700 - 1701", *English Historical Review,* LXX1, 223-246.

13   Bennett and Parsons, op. cit., 209; Register ..., 6-10.

14   Porritt, E., *The Unreformed House of Commons,* I, 159.

15   A.A., 1/3/21.

16   Merewether and Stephens, op. cit., II, 1401.

17   A.A., 20m50/8.

18   *The Corporation of Andover, 1599 - 1835* (Andover Archives), 10.

19   *Burke's Peerage,* sub Cope.

20   *Burke's Peerage,* sub Hertford.

21   Sedgwick, R., *The House of Commons 1715 - 1754,* I, 597; Flinn, M. W. (ed.), *The Lawbook of the Crowley Ironworks,* XVIII; Flinn, M. W., *Men of Iron: the Crowleys and the early iron industry,* 31, 55, 59-61, 68.

22   Beatson, R., *A Chronological Register of the Houses of the British Parliament from .... 1707 to .... 1807,* I, 174.

23   Keeler, op. cit., 336; *V.C.H., Hants,* IV, 148, 149.

Shortly after the death of Queen Anne, the Jacobite threat to the new Hanoverian dynasty led to the maximum life of Parliament being increased from three years to seven by the Septennial Act of 1715. During the eighteenth and early nineteenth centuries, the Wallops, with their principal seat at Hurstbourne Park nearby, normally exercised the right of nominating one Burgess for Andover. In 1715, the head of the family himself, John Wallop (1690 - 1762), was elected and was also able to nominate one member for Whitchurch. He was created Viscount Lymington in 1720 and Earl of Portsmouth in 1743; before this he had been MP for the county from 1715 to 1720 (electing not to sit for Andover) and Lord Lieutenant of Hampshire from 1733.[1]

To fill the seat left vacant at Andover in 1715 he nominated James Brudenell (c1687 - 1746) who was returned at a by-election held on 1st April 1715. Brudenell was the younger brother of the third Earl of Cardigan, a Tory, but was himself a Whig. The two brothers had been converted from Catholicism to the Church of England by their cousin, the Duke of Shrewsbury, while living in Rome. James married Susan Burton, the daughter of a rich London merchant of North Luffenham, Lincolnshire, where he too lived. He represented Chichester from 1713 to 1715 and again from 1734 to 1746, in the interest of his brother-in-law, the Duke of Richmond. He held a number of lucrative positions, being successively Master of the Jewel Office (£450 pa), Commissioner of the Board of Trade (£1,000 pa), Groom of the Bedchamber (£500 pa) and Gentleman of the Horse (£250 pa), while his wife was Woman of the Bedchamber to the Queen (£300 pa). Not surprisingly he voted consistently for the government of the day. The second and third of these appointments, in accordance with the Act for the Security of Her Majesty's person and Government, 1708, necessitated by-elections at Andover in 1716 and 1720.

Brudenell played little part in parliamentary affairs though in November 1722 he attracted attention when "there was a very large Committee, and Mr. Brudenell, for want of a seat got into the Speaker's Chair, and though all the House took notice of it as well as the Chairman, yet he continued there the whole committee with great confidence, a thing never done before".[2]

His fellow member in 1715 was William Guidott (c1671 - 1745), who had been elected previously in 1708, 1710 and 1713 and was to be re-elected in 1722, 1730 and 1734. He was descended from a Florentine family which settled in Southampton in the sixteenth century, and was Steward of Andover, like his father, another William, and later its Recorder. He lived at Laverstoke and Preston Candover, having married Patience Soper, the heiress of the latter place, and had been educated at Oxford and Lincoln's Inn. He acted as agent for the Duke of Marlborough and was sued by the Duchess for nearly £10,000 which he was accused of embezzling, over £6,000 of which he had to repay.[3]

In 1727, Polling Day being 2nd August, he failed to hold his seat when the voting went as follows:

James Brudennell	22
Charles Colyear	14
William Guidott	10
Matthew Skinner	
Abel Ketelby	

After the election Colyear wrote to Walpole explaining what had happened: "The Corporation of Andover having for some elections past made Lord Lymington the compliment of taking his recommendation for one Member, who was Mr. Brudenell, and Mr. Guidott always stood upon his own interest, but by some accident or other having disobliged a majority of the voters, they were determined to elect another in his room, upon which Mr. Hoare the banker was applied to and had I not luckily intervened, they had determined that night to accept him. But the Corporation being rather inclined for the Whig interest approved of me and dropped Mr. Hoare yet were fixed in the resolutions at all events to set aside Mr. Guidott".[4]

The other two unsuccessful candidates were Tories. Abel Ketelby (c1676 - 1744) was a Tory lawyer who defended some of the Jacobites after the Fifteen Rebellion, and was MP for Ludlow from 1722 to 1727.[5] Matthew Skinner, another lawyer, was Recorder of Oxford and represented the City from 1734 to 1738 in the interest of the Earl of Abingdon, but went over to the Whigs and was made Chief Justice of Chester as a reward in 1738.[6]

The two Tories petitioned Parliament on the familiar grounds that the resident freemen had the right to vote and that 53 of these were their supporters. The freemen also petitioned against the restriction of the franchise, "whose numbers being so few, a majority of them have made corrupt bargains and divided considerable sums of money among themselves for their votes of Members to serve for the borough in the present Parliament".

On 19th February 1727, the Bailiff informed the corporation that he had been ordered by the Committee of Privileges and Elections to furnish Colyear with charters, records and Court books, and permission was accordingly given to a solicitor called Tirrell (himself an ex-member of the corporation and a violent opponent of the existing oligarchy) to make a search on Colyear's behalf, in order to defend his seat. However, both petitions were withdrawn, so his defence became unnecessary.[7]

The feeling in the town on this subject is reflected in an entry in the Minute Book of the Haberdashers' Company of Andover on 23rd October 1733:

> "It is agreed by this Society this day met that the Chamberlayne of this Company Doe forthwith pay to the Master Warden thereof the sum of Seventeen pounds, part of the Stock in hand of this Company, to advise with Councel and for other purposes towards trying the right of Electing a Bayliff for the Borough of Andover forsaid, And also the right of Chusing two Burgesses to represent the said Borough in the next Parliament, it being presumed that the ffreemen of the Company have votes for such Bayliff and Burgesses".[8]

The successful candidate in 1727, Charles Colyear, Viscount Milsington (1700 - 1785), who had been MP for Chipping Wycombe in 1726, was the only son of David, first Earl of Portmore, by Catherine Sedley, the mistress of James II. He succeeded to his father's peerage in 1730 and William Guidott regained his seat at the subsequent by-election.[9]

John Pollen (c 1702 - 1775), member for Andover from 1734 to 1754, was the son of the MP of the same name elected in 1689 and 1690.

Educated at Winchester, Oxford and Lincoln's Inn, he was a professional lawyer, a confirmed Whig, and a member of the corporation from 1729. His appointment as a Welsh Judge in 1742 forced him to vacate his seat but he was re-elected at the subsequent by-election. He later applied for the Chief Justiceship of the Circuit and obtained it in 1753. In the election of 1741 he polled 9 votes, against 12 for John Wallop, 8 for William Guidott, and 1 for John Pugh.[10]

John Wallop (1718 - 1749), who was educated at Winchester and Oxford, was elected for Andover in 1741 and 1747. He was the eldest son of the first Earl of Portsmouth and was styled Lord Lymington after 1743, but died during his father's lifetime.[11]

His death in 1749 led to a by-election in which John Griffin Griffin obtained 17 votes to the one cast for Francis Blake Delaval, who nevertheless lodged a petition against the result but subsequently withdraw it.[12] Griffin (1719 - 1797), a professional soldier who ended as a Field Marshal, was born Whitwell and changed his name by Act of Parliament in 1749 on receiving the Saffron Walden estate of his aunt Elizabeth, wife of the first Earl of Portsmouth. It was his uncle who in 1749 secured his election at Andover, a seat he continued to hold until 1784 when he became a peer as Lord Howard de Walden. He had earlier, in 1766, applied to Pitt the Elder for a peerage but without success. In 1785, he was also made Lord Braybrooke by Pitt the Younger. As an MP he was independent but normally supported the government, though he opposed the official policy relating to the American Colonies.[13]

Sir Francis Blake Delaval (1727 - 1771), who had been unsuccessful in the 1749 by-election, was returned for Andover in 1754 and 1761. Educated at Westminster and Christchurch, Oxford, he was a member of the Northumberland family of Seaton Delaval, a man of fashion whose financial and other troubles involved him in a good deal of disrepute. The Duke of Newcastle opposed his election in 1754 but in 1760 tried to enlist the support of the Earl of Portsmouth on his behalf, only to meet a rebuff. "When I recommended Major-General Griffin to my friends at Andover", Portsmouth replied, "I promised them that I would not interfere further in the election, so that your Grace sees the impossibility of my serving Mr. Delaval". According to a not very probable story, Delaval owed his election in 1754 to firing off a culverin filled with five hundred golden sovereigns; surely a waste of money when only the twenty-four members of the corporation possessed the vote.[14] Delaval was, in fact, the sort of character to whom "good stories" easily became attached. Another of these, in connection with his electoral defeat in 1768, relates that he was subsequently sued by his attorney, who on his behalf had invited both the Mayor and Corporation, and the Colonel and officers of a regiment stationed nearby, to a dinner in Andover, the invitations apparently coming from the other party concerned. When the ruse was discovered the attorney was thrown out of the window and his legs consequently broken. Among the charges included in his account to Delaval, therefore, was one of £500 for being thrown out of the George Inn, Andover.[15]

In the election of 1761 Griffin came top of the poll with 19 votes, Delaval second with 12, and Benjamin Lethieullier, third with 5. In 1768, however, the last two positions were reversed, Griffin remaining first with 17 votes, but Lethieullier next with 15, and Delaval bottom with 9.[16]

Benjamin Lethieullier, of Belmont, Middlesex, and Middleton, Hampshire (1729 - 1797) was the son of a director of the Bank of England. His mother, Sarah Lascelles, had lately married Joseph Iremonger of Wherwell, and it was in the Iremonger interest that he sat for Andover. He received additional support from his brother-in-law, Sir Matthew Fetherstonhaugh (c1714 - 1774), who had himself contested Andover in 1754, resolved "to try what his friends can do for him", but had been unsuccessful in spite of the backing of the Duke of Newcastle and Joseph Iremonger. Fetherstonhaugh wrote to Newcastle in 1768: "I am going up tomorrow morning to the Duke of Grafton to endeavour to prevent his proceeding to oppose my brother Leithieullier at Andover, where the Duke of Northumberland has engaged him to use his influence, and has joined his own to it, to bring in if possible Sir Francis Delaval. But whether his Grace will I am doubtful, though it will not I believe signify, as I think my brother is pretty sure; but he has desired me to speak to the Duke about it". Fetherstonhaugh's confidence proved to be justified.

In 1774, a contested election showed an increase in the strength of the

Iremonger influence with Lethieullier top of the poll with 18 votes, Griffin second with 13, and John Pollen, son of the MP of 1734 - 1754, third with 7.[17]

Lethieullier does not appear to have spoken in debates but was an active committee member and played a considerable part in the proceedings leading to the launching of the Andover Canal.[18]

Some idea of the political situation in Andover in the late eighteenth century is given by a letter from Miss Iremonger, written from Wherwell on 13th December 1790, to her friend Miss Heber, about the ball "given by my uncle Lethieullier & his Brother Member":

> "The Andover Ball which followed, about which you have interested yourself sufficiently to ask for an account of, had not any other recommendation to me but as an act of Duty indispensable, for I quite hate the sort of thing & was not in my element again till it was over. Could I suppose it would have given you pleasure to have made one of the number I am sure I should have wished you there, but you have raised ideas of it beyond any thing it deserves for it was confin'd entirely to the two families who support an interest there, Lord Portsmouth's and my Father's, & the town of Andover. Little indeed therefore is there to relate but that the Corporation was gratified & in good humour, & that I was delighted to find myself at full liberty to come home at two in the morning & left my Niece, my elder Brother's daughter, with her Father & Mother to take care of her, dancing till four".[19]

When Griffin was elevated to the House of Lords in 1784, Lord Portsmouth nominated his brother-in-law, William Fellowes (c1726 - 1804) of Ramsey Abbey, Huntingdon. He was returned unopposed and re-elected in 1790, but there is no record of his having spoken in the House of Commons except that he presented the report of the Select Committee set up in connection with the proposed Andover Canal in 1789.[20] He had previously represented Ludlow and was the first cousin of Coulson Fellowes of Eggesford and Ramsey Abbey. He was a supporter of Pitt the Younger.[21]

In 1796 Fellowes was succeeded by Coulson Wallop (1774 - 1807), the third son of the Earl of Portsmouth, who got his Christian name from his grandfather, Coulson Fellowes. He made no mark in the House of Commons and in 1800 he was described as "little better than an idiot"! He had the misfortune to go to France during the Peace of Amiens in 1802 and when war was declared again he was imprisoned and died in captivity at Verdun.[22] The election of 1796 was managed by Sir Henry Fetherstonhaugh on behalf of Lettieullier and the Wallop family, in collaboration with Ralph Etwall senior, the deputy Steward. Thomas Assheton Smith also stood, but failed to secure election.[23]

At the next election Coulson Wallop's place was taken by his elder brother, the second son, Newton Wallop (1722 - 1854), so called after his mother, the niece of Sir Isaac Newton. He took the name and arms of Fellowes in 1794 on succeeding to the estates of his maternal uncle, Henry Arthur Fellowes, and remained MP for Andover until 1820 besides being its Steward. Both his brothers were feeble minded and after 1814 his elder brother's conduct was a source of anxiety, though he was not certified until 1823. Newton Wallop made no speeches in the House, though he was a regular attender. In 1810 he voted for Parliamentary reform and in 1812 for Catholic relief.[24] In 1853 he succeeded as the fourth Earl of Portsmouth. His son, Henry Arthur Wallop Fellowes (1797 - 1847), was in turn elected in 1831 and 1833, being regarded as a Reformer and in favour of the ballot.[25]

In 1797, on the death of Benjamin Lethieullier, his seat was taken by Thomas Assheton Smith (1752 - 1828), of Tidworth, the collateral descendant of Speaker Smith mentioned earlier, thus reviving "a virtually extinct interest".[26] He had been defeated the previous year but Joshua Iremonger now made no objection to his candidature.[27] He remained MP until he retired in 1821 in favour of his son, Thomas Assheton Smith the younger (1776 - 1856), who retained the seat until 1831, the eve of the Great Reform Act. The latter was educated at Eton and Corpus Christi College, Oxford, and was devoted to sport in a variety of forms, including cricket, yachting and hunting, continuing the last named into his eightieth year. After losing his seat in Andover he was from 1832 to 1841 MP for Caernarvonshire, where his family owned extensive slate mines. In politics he was a strong Tory. In 1832 he raised a corps of Yeomanry at his own expense to combat the riots which took place in favour of Parliamentary Reform.[28]

43

Thomas Assheton Smith, the younger

From 1820 to 1831 the Assheton Smiths were associated with Sir John Walter Pollen, Bt (c1784 - 1863), the grandson of the Welsh judge who had represented the borough in the eighteenth century and whose father had been Bailiff of Andover. He was re-elected in 1835 and 1837, on the first occasion "in opposition to Mr. Nightingale, who stood the first contest the borough has witnessed for many years".[29] It was Pollen and the younger Assheton Smith who aroused the anger of Cobbett in October 1822, on one of his Rural Rides. Referring to Tidworth, he wrote:

"This is the seat of Asheton Smith; and the fine coursing that I once saw there I should have called to recollection with pleasure if I could have forgotten the hanging of the men at Winchester last Spring for resisting one of Smith's game-keepers! This Smith's son and a Sir John Pullen are the members for Andover. They are chosen by the Corporation. One of the Corporation, an Attorney, named Etwall, is a Commissioner of the Lottery, or something in that way. It would be a curious thing to ascertain how large a portion of the public services is performed by the voters in Boroughs and their relations. These persons are singularly kind to the nation. They not only choose a large part of the representation of the people; but they come in person, or by deputy, and perform a very considerable part of the public services".

Again: " ... to return to the above-mentioned hanging at Winchester (a thing never to be forgotten by me) James Turner, aged 28 years, was accused of assisting to kill Robert Baker, game-keeper to Thomas Asheton Smith Esq., in the parish of South Tidworth. I deem his hanging at Winchester worthy of general attention, and particularly at this time, when the aristocracy near Andover ... was ... endeavouring, at the late meeting in Andover, to persuade people, that they the aristocrats wished to keep up the price of corn for the sake of labourers whom Sir John Pullen (Asheton Smith's son's present colleague and member for Andover) called 'Poor Devils' and who, he said, had 'hardly a rag to cover them!' Amicable feeling, tender-hearted souls! Cared not a straw about rents! Did not; oh, no! did not care even about the farmers! It was only for the sake of the poor, naked devils of labourers, that the colleagues of young Thomas Asheton Smith cared ...' They 'have never ... been half so famous, they and this Corporation, whom they represent, as they have been since the meeting which they held here, which ended in their defeat and confusion'".[30]

This is a reminder of the bitterness of political feeling aroused in the last years of the unreformed Parliament.

The Ralph Etwall referred to by Cobbett was the second of three generations to bear the same name, and like his father was Bailiff, Deputy Steward and Town Clerk of Andover.[31] He was the father of the MP who held the seat from 1831 to 1847 in the Liberal interest. Educated at Trinity, Cambridge, and Lincoln's Inn, Ralph Etwall the Third devoted most of his time to field sports, and these, added to the expenses of his election contests, landed him so heavily in debt that he had to leave the country. He was described in 1833 as being "of Whig principles, inclining to Radicalism. He was first elected for the borough, in which he has sufficient interest to be called one of its Patrons, in 1831, and voted for the Reform Act". In 1838 it was noted that he was "in favour of the repeal of the Corn Laws and short parliaments".[32]

On the eve of Parliamentary Reform Andover was typical of those boroughs whose "patrons were able to have their way so long as they were careful to oblige and to flatter the freemen and to provide for the needs of the borough". It was one of 124 corporation boroughs which "may be eliminated from serious consideration when attempting to assess the relevance of party influences", and no poll was held there after 1796. It was also one of a smaller number of boroughs "in which party activity, if it had ever existed, had ceased to exist by the late eighteenth century". At the same time the sale of votes had allegedly "become so sophisticated ... that the voters employed an agent to sell their seat for the highest bidder".[33]

Notes:

1   Sedgwick, op. cit., II, 507.
2   ibid, I, 498; Wake, J., *The Brudenells of Deane*, 189-191, 195, 219, 258-259.

46

3   Sedgwick, op. cit., II, 89; *V.C.H., Hants*, II, 373.

4   Sedgwick, op. cit., II, 1248-9.

5   ibid., II, 189.

6   ibid., II, 425.

7   ibid., I, 249; *The Corporation of Andover*, 11; Register ...; 10-11.

8   Gross, op. cit., II, 348.

9   Sedgwick, op. cit., I, 597.

10   ibid., II, 359-60; I, 249; Bennett and Parsons, op. cit., 4; Earney, op. cit., 11; Register ..., 11.

11   Sedgwick, op. cit., II, 508.

12   ibid., I, 249; Beatson, op. cit., I, 174.

13   Namier, Sir L., and Brooke, John, *The House of Commons, 1754 - 1790*, II, 553-5; *D.N.B.* sub Griffin.

14   Namier and Brooke, op. cit., II, 309-310; Askham, F., *The Gay Delavals*, 76, 120, 125; Earney, op. cit., 1-2.

15   Grego, John, *A History of Parliamentary Elections and Electioneering in the Old Days*, 228-9.

16   Namier and Brooke, op. cit., I, 293.

17   ibid., II, 422; III, 37-8, I, 293.

18   *The Andover Canal* (Andover Local Archives, No. 1), ed. Spaul, J. E. H.

19   Bamford, F., (ed.), *Dear Miss Heber*, 79, 94-5.

20   Namier and Brooke, op. cit., II, 418; *The Andover Canal*, 16.

21   Thorne, op. cit., III, 736.

22   ibid., V, 472.

23   ibid., II, 182.

24   ibid., III, 734.

25   *Burke's Peerage* sub Portsmouth, Earl of; *Register* .... 12-13; Dod, 1833, 111.

26   Thorne, op. cit., II, 182.

27   ibid.

28   *D.N.B.* sub Smith, T. A.; Earney, op. cit., 8-10.

29   *Burke's Peerage* sub Pollen; Register ..., 12-13. Dod, 1838, 153.

30   Cobbett, W., *Rural Rides*, I, 110; II, 467-8, 479.

31   *Register* ..., 10-13.

32   Earney, op. cit., 2-4; Dod, 1833, 109; Dod, 1838, 107.

33   O'Gorman, op. cit. 39, 40, 42, 343-4, 401, citing Oldfield, T., *A Representative History of Great Britain and Ireland*, V, 179.

One of the forms which the agitation in favour of Reform took in Andover was the drawing up of a petition to Parliament claiming yet again that the Corporation had usurped the right of election from the "commonalty" as a whole. This was to have been presented to the House of Commons by Brougham but his elevation to the office of Lord Chancellor made this no longer possible. The townspeople consulted Serjeant Merewether, a leading authority and joint author of "The History of Boroughs", and he concluded that they had a good case but no chance of winning it owing to the Last Determinations Act 1729, which gave the force of law to the most recent judgment of the House of Commons in cases concerning the Borough franchise.[1] The issue became an academic one with the passing of the Great Reform Bill in 1832 which enfranchised householders paying £10 a year or more in rent. The effect of this measure varied from place to place. In London it was a comparatively low rent, and most householders gained the vote, but in the provinces the effect was less sweeping. In Andover, it is true, the number of electors was multiplied by ten, from 24 to 246, but even so it remained one of only 16 boroughs with less than 260 registered electors. In addition to the £10 householders, seventeen freemen qualified under the old franchise and retained their votes; all but three of these qualified also under the new. The population of the borough in 1831 was 4,748, and with the addition of the parish of Knight's Enham and the tithing of Foxcott, assigned to it by the Boundary Act, this was raised to 4,953. In the old borough there were 966 houses, of which 318 were worth £10 per annum, while the new contained over one thousand houses, of which 325 were worth £10 pa. The assessed taxes rose from £1,891 to £1,930.[2]

A Select Committee recorded the expenses of the 1833 election at Andover, which totalled £157.8s.9d., including £35.1s.6d. for "Ringers, band, bellmen, gaoler, beadle and Serjeants-at-Mace", and £29.8s.6d. for "Gratuity to band and to men for drawing in and chairing the members". The expenses incurred in drawing up the electoral register amounted to £11.4s.10d. A rather curious footnote records: "The poor-rates were the funds from which the expenses paid by the overseers of the poor of the Parish of Andover were defrayed, as the shillings paid by electors on being registered were not sufficient for that purpose by more than one-half, as most of them refused

William Cubitt, 1857
(T.L. Atkinson after Sir Francis Grant)

payment". The cost of special constables for the two days' polling was £5.10s.[3]

The Reform Bill made no immediately discernible difference to the sort of candidate elected at Andover. Fellowes, Etwall and Pollen held the two seats between them from 1832 till 1841, and even then the new name to appear was that of Lord William Paget (1803 - 1873), a Captain in the Royal Navy and second son of the first Marquess of Anglesey who, as Lord Uxbridge, commanded the cavalry at Waterloo.[4] Of these four MP's, only Pollen stood as a Conservative. In 1847, however, Isaac Newton Fellowes, nephew of the third Earl of Portsmouth and himself ultimately the fifth Earl (1825 - 1891), came third in the poll: an unprecedented defeat at Andover for a member of the Wallop family.[5]

In 1852, C. R. Dod noted that Andover, whose inhabitants were "chiefly engaged as malsters, in the manufacture of shags for silk hats, shalloons, etc., and in the supply generally of an agricultural district", still had among its constituents six of the surviving freemen. The number of "£10 householders within Andover, Foxcote, and Knight's Enham" had decreased from 322, at the time of the Reform Act, to 222 in 1847, and the number of registered electors from 246 to 241 in 1852. Under the heading "Influence" Dod commented: "The Hon. Mr. Newton Fellowes (as heir to the estates of the Earl of Portsmouth who is insane) together with the Pollen family, retain only a portion of the influence which they formerly enjoyed".[6]

One of the two successful candidates in 1847, H. Beaumont Coles (1794 - 1862), stood as a Protectionist in this, the first election to follow the repeal of the Corn Laws, and was re-elected as a Conservative in 1852 and 1861, but defeated in 1857. He was a barrister by profession, having studied at Gray's Inn, and had a house in Portman Square. He was "opposed to the endowment of the Roman Catholic Clergy".[7]

The other candidate, William Cubitt (1791 - 1863), represented Andover as a Liberal Conservative from 1847 until his death, with the exception of the eighteen months between July 1861 and December 1862, when he unsuccessfully contested the City of London. Born in

Norfolk, he spent four years in the Navy before learning the building trade from his brother Thomas. He became Sheriff of London in 1847, Alderman in 1851 and was twice elected Lord Mayor. He raised half a million pounds for the relief of distress and when he died at Penton Lodge muffled bells were rung in more than fifty churches.[8] His seat was filled in November 1863 by his son-in-law, William Henry Humphery (1827 - 1909), son of an Alderman of London, who was re-elected in 1865 and created a baronet in 1868. He was educated at Winchester, Wadham and the Inner Temple, and had many sporting interests, including football, hunting and rowing. He was High Sheriff of Hampshire in 1873 and a Lieutenant Colonel in the Volunteers. He was described in 1865 as being "not opposed to moderate alterations so as to meet the requirements of the age; but against 'rash changes'; opposed to 'weak and illjudged interference in foreign politics'".[9]

Sir William Humphery, Bt. K.C.B.

Humphery having accepted the Chiltern Hundreds, a by-election on 11th February 1867 led to the return of Sir John Burgess Karslake, QC, (1821 - 1881), Attorney General in the Conservative administrations of Derby and Disraeli. Son of a solicitor, he was educated at Harrow and the Middle Temple, became a Bencher of his Inn in 1861, and Solicitor General in 1866. He was out of Parliament from 1868 till 1873, when he represented Huntingdon, and became a Privy Councillor in 1876. He was "in favour of the Army and Navy being maintained in a state of efficiency".[10]

The Hon. Dudley Francis Fortescue (1820 - 1909), third son of the second Earl Fortescue, was MP from 1857 to 1874. He was a Commissioner in Lunacy, Deputy Lieutenant of Devonshire and Waterford, and High Sheriff of Waterford. His election at Andover represented a last triumph for the old Wallop connection, for his wife was Lady Camilla Eleanor, daughter of the fourth Earl of Portsmouth. He was a Liberal and favoured "a wider and more equitable basis" for the franchise.[11]

In 1867 the Second Reform Act extended the franchise to householders in boroughs, and the Andover electorate increased to 774 in 1868, 792 in 1874 and 868 in 1880.[12] By the Complementary Act redistributing seats, 35 boroughs with a population between five and ten thousand lost one member each, and Andover was one of these.[13]

For most of the time between 1832 and 1867 Andover had divided its seats between the two main parties. For the last three elections in its history it followed the general trend of the country, returning a Liberal in 1868, a Conservative in 1874, and a Liberal again in 1880. The successful Conservative candidate was Captain (later Colonel) Henry Wellesley (1846 - 1900), grandson of the great Duke of Wellington, who had been defeated by Fortescue in 1868 but now turned the tables to win by 395 to 259. He was himself defeated in the last Andover election by 405 to 364. In 1884 he succeeded his uncle Arthur as third Duke of Wellington.[14]

The winner in Andover's last election was Francis William Buxton (1847 - 1910), a Liberal. He was the seventh son of Sir E. N. Buxton, and educated at Trinity College, Cambridge and Lincoln's Inn. He was a

Col. Henry Wellesley, 3rd Duke of Wellington

Director of the Union Bank of London, a Public Works Loan Commissioner, and Treasurer of the Royal Economic Society, his interests being mainly in social, political and educational questions, as well as sport.[15]

In 1884, Gladstone passed the Third Reform Act. This was coupled with the Redistribution of Seats Act 1885, by which Andover, together with other boroughs with less than 15,000 inhabitants, ceased to be a separate Parliamentary constituency. Its population had increased comparatively slowly in the nineteenth century, from 5,259 in 1831 to 5,744 in 1871, and in a utilitarian age this no longer seemed large enough to justify representation on its own. In January 1886, when the new Parliament met, almost for the first time since 1586 the Speaker could no longer call upon the Member for Andover.

As a result of the growth of its population in the 1960s, Andover in 1983 became once more the centre of a Parliamentary constituency, but this, with an astonishing insensitivity to historical tradition, was called "North West Hampshire", and the name of the borough which had returned members for three hundred years was not revived, although smaller towns such as Romsey were thus identified. A further opportunity was lost in 1995, and this led the sitting Member, Sir David Mitchell, to comment on "what a thoroughly bad job (had) been done by the Boundary Commission. They should have created an Andover seat and left the villages which look to the town with it".[16] Perhaps a future review will rectify the matter.

Notes:

1   A.A., Shaw's Notebook, E.
2   Philbin, J. H., *Parliamentary Representation*, 1832.
3   Gash, N., *Politics in the Age of Peel*, 75-6, 96, 100, 114; P.P. 1833, XXVII, 91; P.P. 1834, IX, Appendix, 17, 59.
4   McCalmont, F. H., *The Parliamentary Poll Book*, 3; *Burke's Peerage* sub Anglesey, Marquess of.
5   *Burke's Peerage* sub Portsmouth, Earl of.
6   Dod, C. R., *Electoral Facts for 1832 to 1852*, 3.
7   Boase, F., *Modern English Biography*, I, 678; Dod, 1847, 149.
8   *D.N.B.* sub Cubitt, William; Earney, op. cit., 15-16: His brother

is the subject of a study by Hermione Hobhouse called *Thomas Cubitt, Master Builder*.

9   *Who was Who*, 1897 - 1915; 361; Dod, 1865, 222.

10   *D.N.B.* sub Karslake, Sir J. B,; Dod, 1868, 236.

11   *Burke's Peerage* sub Fortescue; Dod, 1865, 193.

12   McCalmont, op. cit., 3.

13   Seymour, Charles, *Electoral Reform in England and Wales*, 539.

14   *Burke's Peerage* sub Wellington, Duke of; McCalmont loc. cit.

15   *Who was Who*, 1897 - 1915, 104.

16   Speech to a Special General Meeting of the North West Hants Conservative Association, 21 July 1995.

APPENDIX A

MEMBERS OF PARLIAMENT FOR ANDOVER 1295 - 1885

A Chronological List, compiled from *Members of Parliament*, Part I, Parliaments of England 1213 - 1702 (Parliamentary Papers 696, 1878) and Part 2, Parliaments of England 1703 - 1837 (Parliamentary Papers 697, 1878) and F. H. McCalmont, The Parliamentary Poll Book (1880).

The dates of the Parliaments are those of assembly and dissolution, and have been taken from the *Handbook of British Chronology* (ed. Powicke and Fryde, second edition, 1961). The same source has provided the places of assembly for the medieval parliaments.

Edward I

27 Nov 1295	Westminster	Johannes Oriold; Richardus Lotyn
20 Jan 1301	Lincoln	No Return
14-21 Oct 1302	Westminster	Johannes de Povynton; Willelmus Lucas
28 Feb-20 Mar 1305	Westminster	Henricus de Morton; Johannes Yarnyne
30 May 1306	Westminster	Johannes Arnoue; Rogerus de Clatford
20 Jan 1307	Carlisle	Johannes Arnoue; Johannes Erchebaud

Edward II

13-16 Oct 1307	Northampton	Ricardus de Marisco; Johannes le Poer
27 Apr-13 May 1309	Westminster	No Return
8 Aug-9 Oct 1311	London	No Return

Dates of Parliament	*Dates of Return*	*Names of Members*

Elizabeth I

15 Oct 1586-23 Mar 1587	13 Oct 1586	James Halley, Esq. Edwin Sandis, Esq.
4 Feb-29 Mar 1589	20 Oct 1588	Henry Reade, Esq. Thomas Temple, Esq.
19 Feb-10 Apr 1593	No Date	Miles Sandes, Esq. Edward Barker, Esq.
24 Oct 1597-9 Feb 1598	1 Oct 1597	Edward Phillips, Esq. Edward Reynolds, Esq.
27 Oct-19 Dec 160120	Oct 1601	Henry Ludlowe, Esq. Nicholas Hyde, Esq.

56

James I

19 Mar 1604-9 Feb 1611	6 Mar 1604	Sir Thomas Jermyn, Knt.
		Thomas Antrobus, gent.
5 Apr-7 Jun 1614	No Date	Richard Venables, gent.
		Peter Noes, gent.
16 Jan 1621-8 Feb 1622	11 Dec 1620	John Sutor, Esq.
		Richard Venables, gent.
(By-Election)	22 Nov. 1621	Robert Wallop, Esq, of Farlye Wallop *vice* Richard Venables deceased.
12 Feb 1624-27 Mar 1625	7 Jan 1624	Robert Wallop, Esq.
		John Shuter, Esq.

Charles I

17 May-12 Aug 1625	29 Apr 1625	Sir Henry Wallop, Knt.
		John Shuter, Esq.
6 Feb-15 Jun 1626	24 Jan 1626	The Right Hon Henry, Lord Pawlett.
		John Shuter, Esq.
17 Mar 1628-10 Mar 1629	29 Feb 1628	Robert Wallop, Esq.
		Ralph Conway, Esq.
13 Apr-5 May 1640	12 Mar 1640	Sir Richard Wynn, Bart.
		Robert Wallop, Esq.
3 Nov 1640-20 Apr 1653	19 Oct 1640	Robert Wallop, Esq.
		Sir Henry Rainsford, Knt.
(By-election)		(Henry Vernon returned as MP but unseated.)
		Sir William Waller *vice* Sir Henry Rainsford, deceased.

Commonwealth

3 Sep 1654-22 Jan 1655		John Dunck, Esq (Sat for Berkshire).
27 Jan-22 Apr 1659	4 Jan 1659	Gabriel Beck, Esq of Westminster.
		Robert Gough, Esq of Vernham's Deane, Co Southampton.

Charles II

25 Apr-29 Dec 1660	20 Apr 1660	John Trott, Esq of Ash, Co Southampton.
		John Collins, Esq of Chute, Co Wiltshire.
8 May 1661-24 Jan 1679	21 Mar 1661	John Collins, Esq, Steward of Andover.
		Sir John Trott, Bart, of Ash, Co Southampton.

By-election	10 Feb 1673	Sir Kingsmill Lucy, Bart, of St Martin's in the Field, Co. Middlesex, *vice* Sir John Trott, Bart, deceased.
By-election	29 Oct 1678	Hon Charles West, elder son and heir of Charles Lord Lawarr, *vice* Sir Kingsmill Lucy, deceased.
6 Mar-12 Jul 1679	11 Feb 1679	Francis Powlett, Esq of Amport, Co Southampton. William Wither, Esq of Manydowne in the parish of Lawrence Wootton, Co Southampton.
21 Mar-28 Mar 1681	4 Mar 1681	Hon Charles West, son and heir apparent of Charles Lord Delawarr. John Collins, Esq.

James II

19 May 1685-2 Jul 1687	9 Mar 1685	Sir John Collins, Knt, Steward of Andover. Colonel Robert Phillips.

William III and Mary II

22 Jan 1689-6 Feb 1690	14 Jan 1689	Francis Powlett, Esq of Amport, within the Hundred of Andover. John Pollen, Esq of Andover.
20 Mar 1690-11 Oct 1695	3 Mar 1690	Hon Francis Powlett, Esq of Amport, within the Hundred of Andover. John Pollen, Esq of Andover.
22 Nov 1695-7 Jul 1698	30 Oct 1695	John Smyth, Esq, a Privy Councillor. Sir Robert Smyth, Bart.
24 Aug 1698-19 Dec 1700	21 Jul 1698	John Smyth, one of the Lords Commissioners of the Treasury and a Privy Councillor. Anthony Henley, Esq of The Grange, Co Southampton.
6 Feb-11 Nov 1701	8 Jan 1701	John Smyth, Esq, Chancellor and Under Treasurer of the Exchequer, one of the Lords of the Treasury, and a Privy Councillor. Francis Sheppherd, Esq of London.
30 Dec 1701-2 Jul 1702	25 Nov 1701	John Smyth, Esq, a Privy Councillor. Francis Sheppherd, Esq of London.

Anne

20 Aug 1702-5 Apr 1705	16 Jul 1702	John Smith, Esq, a Privy Councillor. Francis Sheppherd, Esq of London.
14 Jun 1705-3 Apr 1708	11 May 1705	John Smith, Esq, PC. Francis Shepheard.
8 Jul 1708-21 Sep 1710	6 May 1708	John Smith, Esq, Chancellor and Under Treasurer of the Court of the Exchequer and Privy Councillor. William Guidott, Esq.
25 Nov 1710-8 Aug 1713	5 Oct 1710	John Smith, Esq of South Tidworth, County of Southampton, a Privy Councillor. William Guidott, Esq, Steward of the Borough of Andover.
12 Nov 1713-15 Jan 1715	25 Aug 1713	William Guidott, Esq, Steward of the Borough of Andover. Sir Ambrose Crowley, Knt, Alderman of the City of London.
By-election	30 Nov 1714	Gilbert Searle, Esq of Testwood, *vice* Sir Ambrose Crowley, Knt, deceased.

George I

17 Mar 1715-10 Mar 1722	29 Jan 1715	John Wallop, Esq of Farley Wallop. William Guidott, Esq.
By-elections	1 Apr 1715	James Brudenell, Esq *vice* John Wallop, Esq, who elected to serve for the County of Southampton.
	3 Apr 1716	James Brudenell, Esq, re-elected after appointment to an office of profit by the Crown.
10 May 1722-5 Aug 1727	21 Mar 1722	William Guidott, Esq. James Brudenell, Esq.

George II

28 Nov 1727-17 Apr 1734	23 Aug 1727	James Brudenell, Esq. Charles Colyear, Esq.
By-elections	20 Jan 1730	William Guidott, Esq, *vice* Charles Colyear, Esq, commonly called Viscount Milsington, called to the Upper House as Earl of Portmore.
	26 May 1730	James Brudenell, Esq, re-elected after appointment to an office of profit by the Crown.

	25 Jun 1733	James Brudenell, Esq, re-elected after appointment to an office of profit by the Crown.
13 Jun 1734-27 Apr 1741	25 Apr 1734	William Guidott, Esq.
		John Pollen, Esq.
25 Jun 1741-18 Jun 1747	5 May 1741	John Wallop, Esq.
		John Pollen, Esq.
By-election	8 Apr 1742	John Pollen, Esq, re-elected after appointment as one of the Justices of the Courts of Carmarthen, Pembroke and Cardigan, and of the town and county of Haverfordwest, and of the county and borough of Carmarthen.
13 Aug 1747-8 Apr 1754	29 Jun 1747	John Wallop, Esq, commonly called Lord Viscount Lymington.
		John Pollen, Esq.
By-election	28 Nov 1749	John Griffin Griffin, Esq, *vice* John Wallop, commonly called Lord Viscount Lymington, deceased.
31 May 1754-20 Mar 1761	16 Apr 1754	John Griffin Griffin, Esq.
		Francis Blake Delaval, Esq.

George III

19 May 1761-11 Mar 1768	30 Mar 1761	Sir John Griffin Griffin, Knt of the Bath.
		Sir Francis Blake Delaval, Knt of the Bath.
10 May 1768-30 Sep 1774	21 Mar 1768	Sir John Griffin Griffin, Knt of the Bath.
		Benjamin Lethieullier, of Middleton, County Southampton.
29 Nov 1774-1 Sep 1780	5 Oct 1774	Sir John Griffin Griffin, Knt of the Bath.
		Benjamin Lethieullier, Esq.
31 Oct 1780-25 Mar 1784	8 Sep 1780	Sir John Griffin Griffin, Knt of the Bath.
		Benjamin Lethieullier, Esq.
18 May 1784-11 Jun 1790	30 Mar 1784	Sir John Griffin Griffin, Knt of the Bath.
		Benjamin Lethieullier, Esq.
By-election	11 Aug 1784	William Fellows, Esq of Ramsey, County Huntingdon, *vice* Sir John Griffin Griffin, Knt of the Bath, called to the Upper House as Lord Howard, Baron Howard of Walden.

10 Aug 1790-20 May 1796	16 Jun 1790	Benjamin Lethieullier, Esq. William Fellowes, Esq.
12 Jul 1796-29 Jun 1802	25 May 1796	Benjamin Lethieullier, Esq. Coulson Wallop, Esq.
By-election	14 Dec 1797	Thomas Assheton Smith, *vice* Benjamin Lethieullier, Esq, deceased.
31 Aug 1802-24 Oct 1806	5 Jul 1802	Thomas Assheton Smith, Esq. Newton Fellowes, Esq.
13 Dec 1806-29 Apr 1807	31 Oct 1806	Thomas Assheton Smith, Esq. Newton Fellowes, Esq.
22 Jun 1807-29 Sep 1812	5 May 1807	Thomas Assheton Smith, Esq. Newton Fellowes, Esq.
24 Nov 1812-10 Jun 1818	6 Oct 1812	Thomas Assheton Smith, Esq. Newton Fellowes, Esq.
4 Aug 1818-29 Feb 1820	18 Jun 1818	Thomas Assheton Smith, Esq. Newton Fellowes, Esq.

George IV

21 Apr 1820-2 Jun 1826	8 Mar 1820	Thomas Assheton Smith, Esq. Sir John Walter Pollen, Bart.
By-election	11 May 1821	Thomas Assheton Smith the younger, Esq, *vice* Thomas Assheton Smith, Esq, who accepted the Stewardship of the Chiltern Hundreds, County Bucks.
25 Jul 1826-24 Jul 1830	9 June 1826	Sir John Walter Pollen, Bart. Thomas Assheton Smith, the younger, Esq.

William IV

14 Sep 1830-23 Apr 1831	3 Aug 1830	Sir John Walter Pollen, Bart. Thomas Assheton Smith, Esq.
14 Jun 1831-3 Dec 1832	2 May 1831	Henry Arthur Wallop Fellowes, Esq. Ralph Etwall the younger, Esq.
29 Jan 1833-29 Dec 1834	10 Dec 1832	Henry Arthur Wallop Fellowes, Esq. Ralph Etwall, Esq.
19 Feb 1835-17 Jul 1837	8 Jan 1835	Ralph Etwall, Esq. Sir John Walter Pollen, Bart.

Victoria

11 Sep 1837-23 Jun 1841	24 Jul 1837	Ralph Etwall, Esq. Sir John Walter Pollen, Bart.

19 Aug 1841-23 Jul 1847	29 Jun 1841	Ralph Etwall, Esq. William Paget, Esq, comonly called Lord William Paget.
21 Sep 1847-1 Jul 1852	29 Jul 1847	Henry Beaumont Coles, Esq of Middleton House, in the parish of Longparish, Co Southampton. William Cubitt, Esq of Bedford Hill, Streatham, Co Surrey.
20 Aug 1852-21 Mar 1857	9 Jul 1852	William Cubitt, Esq of Bedford Hill, Balham, Co Surrey. Henry Beaumont Coles, Esq of Middleton House, in the parish of Longparish, Co Southampton.
30 Apr 1857-23 Apr 1859	28 Mar 1857	William Cubitt, Esq of Penton Lodge, Co Southampton. Dudley Francis Fortescue, Esq of Summerville, Co Waterford,Ireland.
31 May 1859-6 Jul 1865	30 Apr 1859	William Cubitt, Esq of Penton Lodge, Co Southampton. Dudley Francis Fortescue, Esq of 17 Grosvenor Square, London.
By-elections	29 Jul 1861	Henry Beaumont Coles, Esq of Middleton House, in the parish of Longparish, Co Southampton, *vice* William Cubitt, Esq (now Lord Mayor of the City of London) who accepted the Stewardship of the Manor of Hempholme, Co York.
	17 Dec 1862	William Cubitt, Esq of Penton Lodge, Co Southampton.
By-election	18 Nov 1863	William Henry Humphery, Esq of Penton Lodge, near Andover, Co Southampton, *vice* Wiliam Cubitt, Esq, deceased.
15 Aug 1865-11 Nov 1868	11 Jul 1865	Dudley Francis Fortescue, Esq of 9 Hertford Street, Mayfair, Co Middlesex. William Henry Humphery, Esq of Penton Lodge, near Andover, Co Southampton.
By-election	11 Feb 1867	Sir John Burgess Karslake, Knt of the Middle Temple, Solicitor General, *vice* William Henry Humphery, Esq, who accepted the Stewardship of the Chiltern Hundreds, Co Bucks.

10 Dec 1868-26 Jan 1874	17 Nov 1868	Dudley Francis Fortescue, Esq of 9 Hertford Street, Mayfair, London, Co Middlesex.
5 Mar 1874-24 Mar 1880	9 Feb 1874	Captain Henry Wellesley of Conholt, Co Wilts.
29 Apr 1880-14 Aug 1885		Francis William Buxton.

APPENDIX B

THE RIGHT OF ELECTION AT ANDOVER IN THE TIME OF THE
UNREFORMED PARLIAMENT
(From the *House of Commons Journal*, X, 701)

The report of the Committee of Privileges and Elections was made to
the House on 1st April 1689 by Colonel Birch, who began by saying
that the question was "Whether the Election lay in the Bailiff, and
select number of Burgesses only; or, in the Populace.

That, for the Petitioners, the Counsel insisted that Andover was an
ancient Borough that used to send Members to Parliament; which
have been chosen by the Populace:

And produced Two Precepts for the Electing of Burgesses, with their
Returns, 33 E I, and 34 E I; but it did not appear, by whom they were
chose; As also, Two Indentures of Return of Burgesses in 30 Eliz. and
39 Eliz. said to be with the Consent of the Corporation, and
Commonality of the Town:

Also, a Writ for Electing of a Burgess for that Town, in the Place of Sir
Henry Rainsford, then lately deceased; with the Return of the same,
Anno 41, under the Seal of the Corporation: Which Return had been
amended and Sir William Waller's Name put in the Place of Sir Henry
Vernon, originally returned.

An order of this House was likewise read, for the referring the Petition
of Sir William Waller, touching the Election, to a Committee.

Richard Butcher, a Witness, said, Sir William Waller in 41, was chosen
by the Populace; for, he said, he heard them cry out *A Waller!* and that
there was a Poll demanded: That he is aged about Sixty Years of Age;
and was then about Fifteen Years of Age.

William Erney, a Witness, aged Sixty-four Years, spake to the like
effect.

Another Witness - That there was a Petition against my Lord
Delaware's son, and Mr. Collins, in Oxford Parliament, upon the Right

of the Populacy; but the Parliament was dissolved before it was determined.

That in Westminster Parliament, Two Years before the Burgesses were chosen by the Select Number: That, for the last Parliament before this, the Town had a Design to assert their Rights, but the Town Clerk threatened then to prosecute them for a Riot if they did.

That for the Sitting Members, the Counsel agreed the Question, but said further That Andover was a Corporation by Prescription; and that the election of Burgesses had always been by the Select Number: They insisted that the Records of E.I showed there were then Members returned; but it did not appear by them who were the Electors.

That they produced an ancient Book of the Corporation; by which it appeared, That several Courts had been held by the Maneloquiums, and an Order made per Senescallum, and 24 for Wardinos 37 H.VI.

That they produced their Charter; which recited, That they had been a Corporation of Time immemorial.

Then were produced Indentures of Return, ff. of 28 Eliz, I Jac., 18 Jac., 21 Jac., 15 Car. I, under the Common Seal.

John Dawling, Edward Cook, John Read, Witnesses, testified, That they had known several Elections; and that all they remembered were by the Select Number.

And that, upon the whole Matter, the Counsel for the Petitioners agreeing, it was a Corporation by Prescription; and it appearing to the Committee, that the Usage of the said Borough had been to choose Burgesses by the Bailiff, and Select Number only; the Committee came to Two Resolutions: Which he read in his Place; and afterwards delivered the same in at the Clerk's Table: Where the same being read, are as followeth:

Resolved, That it is the opinion of this Committee, That the Right of Election of Burgesses to serve in Parliament for the Borough of Andover in the County of Southampton, is in the Bailiff, and Select Number of Burgesses, only.

Resolved, That it is the Opinion of this Committee, That Francis Powlett and John Pollen, Esquires, are duly elected Burgesses to serve in this present Parliament, for the Borough of Andover."

These resolutions were then endorsed by the House, and were accepted as decisive in future election disputes concerning the right to vote in Andover.

APPENDIX C

ELECTION EXPENSES AT ANDOVER IN 1834
Extract from the *Report of the Select Committee on Election Expenses,* P.P., 1834, IX, Appendix, p. 17:

ANDOVER

An Account of the Charges, Fees, etc., made against Candidates at the last General Election:

	£	s.	d.
Messenger with Precept	1	1	0
Under Sheriff's Fees	12	12	0
Town-Clerk's fees for trouble in conducting the election, drawing and engrossing the return and counterpart, and for stamps and parchment, 25*l.* each member.	50	0	0
Ringers, band, bellman, gaoler, beadle and Serjeants-at-Mace	35	1	6
Gratuity to band and to men for drawing in and chairing the members	29	8	6
Expenses of printing addresses, etc.	18	9	9
Expenses of the hustings	10	16	0
	£157	8	9

Ibid. p. 59 (Expenses for register of electors)

	£	s.	d.
Sundry expenses in preparing lists of voters, and posting such lists when printed on the doors of the church, chapels, and other places of public worship.	3	13	6
Paid printer for plan of list of voters		9	0
Printer's charges for paper and printing of 150 lists of voters for the borough	2	10	0

These items were charged to the overseers of

the Parish of Andover and paid by them.

Town Clerk's charges for correspondence with W. P.
Taunton and G. Warry, Esqs. (revising barristers),
and making copies of notices of time of their
holding open courts, to be affixed to the doors
of the church, chapels, and other places of public
worship; and paid man for affixing same   1   19   0

Charged to the revising barristers (W. P. Taunton
and G. Warry, Esqrs.) and paid by them.

Town Clerk's charges for making copy of list of
voters, as revised by the barristers, under the
Act 2 Gul. 4, c. 45, as the register of voters,
to be kept for the said borough, eight sheets   1   6   8

Making another fair copy for use, if wanted   1   6   8

Paid by the overseers of the poor of the Parish
of Andover

                                      £11   4   10

There were no copies of the register printed for that year.

The poor-rates were the funds from which the expenses paid by the overseers of
the poor of the Parish of Andover were defrayed, as the shillings paid by electors
on being registered were not sufficient for that purpose by more than one-half, as
most of them refused payment.

The above account does not include any expenses incurred for printing notices and
lists of county voters, in respect of property situate in the parish of Andover. The
overseers of the poor of this Parish paid 5l. 10d. for the expenses of special constables, during the two days polling at Andover for members of the northern division
of the County of Hants.

21 February 1834

                                      WM. PITMAN.
                                        (Bailiff)

APPENDIX D

AN EIGHTEENTH CENTURY POLL AT ANDOVER (1727)
(Reproduced by permission of the Hampshire Record Office, reference 20 M 50/15).

Corporation of Andover, poll for Members of Parliam. taken 23 Aug. 1727:

The Candidates are

	The Hon[ble] Charles Colyear Esq[r]	The Hon[ble] James Brudenell, Esq[r]	Wm Guidott Esq[r]
Mr. Ab[m] Treacle, Bayliff		—	—
W[m] Guidott Esqr		—	—
John Bray	—	—	
George Noyes Sen		—	—
Julius Somborne		—	—
W[m] Bulcher	—	—	
John Cook	—	—	
Roger Bird	—	—	
Tho[s] Woodman		—	—
Rob[t] Hillman		—	—
Henry Silverthorne	—	—	
Isaac King	—	—	
W[m] Smith	—	—	
Richard Wright	—	—	
Daniel Flower	—	—	
Rich[d] Widmore		—	—
Robt. Noyes	—	—	
Roger Hall	—	—	
John Bray Jun[r]	—	—	
John Cook Jun	—	—	
George Noyes Jun		—	—
Joseph Percy		—	—
Robt Longman	—	—	
Abr. Treacle Jun		—	—
	14	24	10

James Brudenell Esq[r] declared duly Elected
Charles Colyear Esq[r] also.

69

LIST OF ELECTORS ON THE ROLL AT ANDOVER IN 1833
(Reproduced by permission of the Hampshire Record Office, reference 20 M 50/17)

[The third column headed "Nature of Qualification" has been omitted, since this is in all cases "House", except numbers 13 and 20 ("Part of a House"); 17, 30, 70, 80, 83, 88, 96, 104, 143, 144, 145, 146, 150, 182, 207 and 210 ("House and Land"), and 133 ("Tan Yard and Storehouses")].

The List of Persons entitled to vote in the Election of Members for the Borough of Andover in respect of Property occupied within the Borough of Andover by virtue of an Act passed in the second year of the Reign of King William the Fourth, entitled "An Act to amend the Representation of the People in England and Wales".

	Christian Name and Surname of each Voter at full length	*Street, Lane or other place in this Parish where the property Number is situate*
1	Adams, John	New Street
2	Allies, Samuel	Chantry Street
3	Adams, Henry	Market Place
4	Alexander, Thomas	King's Head Street
5	Alder, John	King's Head Street
6	Adams, Thomas	Rack Close
7	Biggs, Thomas	Enham
8	Barnes, George	Bridge Street
9	Boyes, Thomas	Queen Inn
10	Barnes, William	High Street
11	Bridger, William Fowler	High Street
12	Bartlett, Thomas	High Street
13	Brewer, William Henry	High Street
14	Bensley, Benjamin	Soper's Lane
15	Bailey, Francis	Bridge Street
16	Baverstock, Thomas	King's Head Street
17	Brackstone, William	Wild Hern
18	Barnaby, Gabriel	New Street
19	Beckley, Thomas	Winchester Street
20	Blunt, Edward Walter	King's Enham
21	Batchelor, Charles	Acre
22	Bussey, John	East Street
23	Baker, James	Market Place
24	Berry, John	King's Head Street
25	Brewer, George	Market Place
26	Bray, George	Soper's Lane
27	Brock, William	King's Head Street
28	Broad, George	Bridge Street
29	Baker, Benjamin Russell	Market Place

30	Crouch, William	New Street
31	Colbrook, Charles	Little London
32	Criswick, Henry	Bridge Street
33	Cole, Robert	New Street
34	Cooper, Thomas	New Street
35	Chevis, Thomas	New Street
36	Collings, Thomas	Winchester Street
37	Callaway, James	Market Place
38	Clarke, Turner Page	Bridge Street
39	Coster, John	King's Head Street
40	Charlton, Joseph	Winchester Street
41	Curtis, John	High Street
42	Cockings, Richard	High Street
43	Criswick, William	High Street
44	Comport, Ebenezer	High Street
45	Cox, Caleb	Soper's Lane
46	Carpenter, John	Roundway Farm
47	Chandler, John	Hatherden
48	Chandler, George	Hatherden
49	Charlton, William	High Street
50	Deering, William	Chantry Street
51	Dymond, Edward Frederick	Priory
52	Deane, William	Barlows Lane
53	Deane, William	New Street
54	Davies, William	High Street
55	Drew, William	High Street
56	Dale, Charles	High Street
57	Deller, Richard	Bridge Street
58	Dowling, Robert	Cold Harbour
59	Drouet, William	High Street
60	Etwall, Ralph	New Street
61	Evans, John, Sen.	Bridge Street
62	Evans, Thomas	Bridge Street
63	Evans, Robert	New Street
64	Earle, Henry	Soper's Lane
65	Emmett, George	High Street
66	Ellen, Joseph	High Street
67	Footner, Richard	Bridge Street
68	Foster, William	Hill House
69	Fouthrop, Thomas	High Street
70	Figges, Thomas Road	New Street and London
71	Godden, John	East Street
72	Godden, John, the Younger	Town Mill
73	Gibbs, William	Soper's Lane
74	Gyatt, Charles	King's Head Street
75	Gue, William	East Street
76	Gilmore, George	Bridge Street
77	Grant, James	High Street

78	Giles, Henry	High Street
79	Garrett, William Wither Pink	High Street
80	Goodall, William	Down House
81	Goddard, William Stanley	New Street
82	Gilbert, William	Marlborough Street
83	Green, William	Hatherden
84	Goddall, John	New Street
85	Grace, William	Foxcott
86	Heath, William Hawkins	King's Head Street
87	Hayes, Edward	East Street
88	Hopkins, Thomas	Charlton
89	Hall, Charles	Rackclose
90	Heath, Thomas	King's Head Street
91	Hopgood, John	Chantry Street
92	Holloway, John	Pitt's Mill
93	Hutchins, Thomas	East Street
94	Holdway, William	Bridge Street
95	Hancock, John	King's Head Street
96	Holdway, John	Dowle's Farm
97	Holdway, Charles	Finckley Farm
98	Holdup, John	High Street
99	Herbert, William	High Street
100	Hellicar, John	High Street
101	Hawkins, Edward	High Street
102	Hawkins, Thomas	High Street
103	Jones, David	Little London
104	Jones, Charles	Little London
105	Jukes, James	King's Head Street
106	Jacob, Frederick	King's Head Street
107	Kellow, John	Woodhouse
108	Knapp, William	Winchester Street
109	King, John Perkins	High Street
110	King, Charles	High Street
111	Lightfood, Joseph	Enham
112	Loscombe, Wintringham	East Street
113	Langstaff, Thomas	Bridge Street
114	Lawes, John	Charlton
115	Leoni, Frederick	High Street
116	Langstaff, William	High Street
117	Laishley, William	Winchester Street
118	Maude, John Lawes	East Street
119	Moore, Thomas	Bridge Street
120	Mundy, Henry	Charlton
121	Marsh, Henry	Hatherden
122	Moody, Thomas, Jun.	High Street
123	Mason, Thomas	High Street
124	Miller, Joseph	High Street
125	Murrell, William	High Street
126	Major, William	High Street

127	Mortimore, John	High Street
128	Marcer, George	High Street
129	Mundy, John	High Street
130	Mundy, Harvey	High Street
131	Margrie, William	High Street
132	Marchment, Thomas	High Street
133	Mortimore, Thomas	Marlborough Street
134	Mann, Thomas	Union Street
135	Morrant, John	King's Head Street
136	Marsh, John	Barlows Lane
137	Murrell, William	Acre
138	Morrell, Thomas	Winchester Street
139	Mills, John	Barlows Lane
140	Matchen, Charles	King's Head Street
141	Matchen, Thomas	East Street
142	Minefy, Henry	King's Head Street
143	Mundy, John	Eastanton
144	Mundy, James	Eastanton
145	Mundy, Hugh	Finkley Farm
146	Mundy, Charles	Bunny's Farm
147	Minefy, Richard	Bridge Street
148	Moore, Robert	Soper's Lane
149	Maidment, John	Winchester Street
150	Munday, Henry	Charlton
151	Newman, Thomas	King's Head Street
152	Nevill, John	Charlton
153	Nurse, John	New Street
154	Pearse, James	Bridge Street
155	Porter, Joseph	Theatre Street
156	Pitman, William	High Street
157	Poore, John	High Street
158	Pitman, Henry	High Street
159	Porter, Charles	Theatre Street
160	Palmer, Henry Boswell	High Street
161	Parker, Thomas	High Street
162	Packer, William	High Street
163	Pool, William	High Street
164	Phillips, Thomas	Rack Close
165	Phillips, William	Chantry Street
166	Perry, Richard	Market Place
167	Prior, Thomas	East Street
168	Pocock, Robert	Eastanton
169	Purchase, Thomas	Bridge Street
170	Reding, William Neale	High Street
171	Rodgers, Charles	King's Head Street
172	Reynolds, Edward	High Street
173	Rout, John	High Street
174	Rumsey, William	High Street
175	Rawlins, Thomas	High Street

176	Rawlins, Thomas, the Younger	High Street
177	Reding, John Camion	Bridge Street
178	Suckling, Nelson	Bridge Street
179	Stokes, William	Winchester Street
180	Sweetapple, William	Hillside Cottage
181	Simpkins, George	Chantry Street
182	Steel, George	Charlton
183	Smith, Clement Frederick	Garrett's Cottage
184	Sutton, Charles	King's Head Street
185	Sutton, James	Bridge Street
186	Searle, George	High Street
187	Scullard, George	High Street
188	Shaw, Samuel	High Street
189	Sweetapple, William	Knight's Enham
190	Smith, William	New Street
191	Smith, William	New Street
192	Thurmur, Thomas	New Street
193	Shipton, James	High Street
194	Swaite, Mark	Charlton
195	Sweetapple, John	Foxcott
196	Todd, John Henry	Bridge Street
197	Tubb, Charles	Antelope Street
198	Titeridge, Thomas	High Street
199	Turner, Charles	High Street
200	Telfer, George	High Street
201	Tayler, Richard	High Street
202	Turner, Charles	New Street
203	Turner, William	New Street
204	Trod, Andrew	Winchester Street
205	Turner, Joseph	King's Head Street
206	Thompson, Henry	Bridge Street
207	Tredgold, Henry	King's Enham
208	Talmage, Abraham	Market Place
209	Tyler, Charles	King's Head Street
210	Tyler, William	Chalk Pits
211	Tredgold, William	High Street
212	Wakeford, Joseph	Cricklade
213	Williams, Charles	High Street
214	Wheeler, Charles	High Street
215	Wheeler, Henry	High Street
216	Wickham, George	High Street
217	Wiltshire, Benjamin	High Street
218	Woodward, John	High Street
219	Wheeler, John	King's Head Street
220	Westlake, Thomas	King's Head Street
221	Watts, Isaac	Chantry Street
222	Westbrook, George	Chantry Street
223	Wallington, Timothy	New Street

224	Windover, John, Sen.	Bridge Street	
225	Windover, John, Jun.	Bridge Street	
226	Westcott, Thomas	Winchester Street	
227	Westcott, George	Winchester Street	
228	Young, George	High Street	
229	Young, John	Hatherden	

The List of Freemen of the Borough of Andover entitled to vote in the Election of a Member or Members for the said Borough.

(Andover is given for "place of abode", except 7 and 16, who lived at Kimpton. The first nine are described as "Approved Men of the Corporation", and the remainder as "Burgesses of the Corporation". Numbers in brackets refer to the previous list).

1	Barnes, George	(8)
2	Criswick, Henry	(32)
3	Etwall, Ralph	(60)
4	Footner, Richard	(67)
5	Godden, John	(71)
6	Maude, John Lawes	(118)
7	Poore, Philip Henry	
8	Pitman, William	(156)
9	Todd, John Henry	(196)
10	Footner, Harry	
11	Heath, William Hawkins	(86)
12	Loscombe, Wintringham	(112)
13	Langstaff, Thomas	(113)
14	Poore, John	(157)
15	Pitman, Henry	(158)
16	Thompson, George	
17	Wakeford, Joseph	(212)

INDEX to the text.

The names of MP's for Andover are followed by the dates of their election.

Carlisle, Parliament at, 1,2
Cecil, Robert, Earl of Salisbury, 8,10
Charlecote, 24
Chichester, 37
Christchurch, 6,8
Chute, 23
Clarke, George, 32
Clatford, Roger de (1306), 2
Cobbett, William, 45
Collins, Sir John (1660, 1661, 1681, 1685), 23-26
Colyer, Charles (1727), later Earl of Portmore, 38-39
Combe, 15
Conway, Francis Seymour, Lord, 34-35
Conway, Ralph (1628), 11
Cope, Sir John, 34-35
Crew, Sir Ranulf, 8
Cromwell, Sir Henry, 21
Cromwell, Oliver, 18,21
Cromwell, Richard, 19-21,24
Crowley, Sir Ambrose (1713), 35
Cubitt, William (1847, 1852, 1857, 1859, 1862), 49-51

Dean, John, 24
Delaval, Sir Francis Blake (1754, 1761), 40-41
Devereux, Robert, Earl of Essex, 8-9
Dod, C. R., 50
Dudley, Robert, Earl of Leicester, 4-6,8-9
Dunch/Dunck, John (1654), 19,21
Dymoke, Edward, 7
Dymoke, Frances, 7
Dysart, Lord, 30

Easton, 9
Eastrop, Hants, 35
Enham, 2
Erchebaud, John (1307), 1
Essex, Earl of (see Devereux)
Etwall, Ralph, snr. 43,45,46
Etwall, Ralph (1831, 1833, 1835, 1837, 1841), 46,50